SIMPLE
SMALL TALK

An Everyday Social Skills Guidebook for Introverts on How to Lose Fear and Talk to New People.

Including Hacks, Questions and Topics to Instantly Connect, Impress and Network.

Gerard Shaw

FREE GIFT

This book includes a bonus booklet. Download may be for a limited time only. All information on how you can secure your gift right now can be found at the end of this book.

TABLE OF CONTENTS

INTRODUCTION

What comes after, "Hello?"

Let me guess how you feel about small talk: You hate it. If you're reading this book, and you're like me, small talk isn't your favorite thing. I'm a guy who struggled with it his whole life. The good news: we're not alone.

Some of the most successful celebrities struggle with small talk. Professional tennis player Naomi Osaka is one of them. Like her, you get anxious and avoid socialization. And that's fine.

It is okay to be awkward with small talk just like Naomi, but it is *not* okay to remain that way forever. Just like I have, you've got to overcome your fears. Think of small talk as a life skill with immense benefits you cannot afford to miss. This skill is essential in helping you build friendships and relationships. That's why I wrote this book.

Unlike books powered by gimmick and offering little to no practical advice, this book is useful. There are *no gimmicks*. The advice is *real*, it is *actionable*, and *you will improve* your speaking skills.

What's more: I think you'll enjoy the process.

Think about when you were younger; try to remember the things you did effortlessly. More often than not, you did those things for the love of them. If you set aside the burden of perfection and learn to enjoy small talk, you'll undoubtedly improve.

The truth is, small talk matters, and it is the first step to most of our social interactions. Small talk is the first step for a job interview, a romantic relationship, making meaningful connections, and having exceptional conversations. You can even generate more sales if that's your line of work.

The world is all about conversations! Humans are social creatures. We all desire connections and a sense of belonging; it has always been this way.

Yet, somehow, isolation and loneliness are prevalent in today's society. Part of the problem is that, as interconnected as we are, we've lost the art of small talk. If you can overcome the challenge of making small talk, you will enjoy the power of human connection in an interconnected world.

After you read this book, which is my hope. You *can* overcome this challenge, and you *will*. As a result, perhaps you can go after your dream job or finally muster up the courage to ask out that person that has captured your attention.

This book was designed to enable you to create more authentic and fulfilling friendships that are valuable to you. However, to enjoy all these benefits, you must be willing to put in the work. Be determined to read and execute the ideas in this book.

As difficult as it may seem to speak with total strangers, that's exactly what this book teaches you to do. It may be painful—but remember the adage: "no pain, no gain" and, of course, "practice makes perfect." Clichés aside, this is the truth. The path to mastering small talk takes a little bit of pain and a lot of practice. Don't worry. I'm here to make the process as painless as possible.

Are you shy? Or probably, Socially awkward? Forget that stuff and read on.

I can't stress it enough. This book is about *action*. You must take action to be better at small talk. There are no shortcuts. Gimmicks don't work.

Now then, what comes after, "Hello?"

This book comes with a FREE booklet on masterminding a winning routine to improve calmness and your level of confidence daily. Head to the bottom of this book for instructions on how you can secure your copy today.

CHAPTER ONE

What Is Small Talk?

We will begin our exploration with the foundation of the discourse: the definition of "small talk". We'll ground it in the simple question: What is small talk?

Small talk is light and informal conversation commonly used when talking to someone you don't know very well. Small talk is also a way to converse at networking and social events to create a connection with new people.

I want you to know everything that pertains to small talk when you are done reading this book, so let us leave nothing to assumption.

In this chapter, I will break down the idea of small talk to its most granular components. You will also take on a fascinating yet important talk exercise that requires you to identify the errors in a small sample talk and correct such mistakes.

So far, our definition of small talk is a bit too specific. It's actually broader than I've suggested. Small talk doesn't relate solely to face-to-face interactions because we live in a digital world. This conversation style also pertains to communication through digital means (online messaging apps and platforms) as well. For example, when you chat with someone for the first time on the WhatsApp platform, when you send a sales email, or when you hop on a live chat with a customer service representative, that's small talk.

Think about small talk as a bonding ritual and a strategy for managing interpersonal distance. With little discussion, people can maintain a positive demeanor around others while connecting with them in a warm approach.

Do you work? Do you own a business, or are you a manager? Even if you are a student, so long you are surrounded by people, you will need to develop small talk skills. How did you become friends with your current *best* friend? You probably met him/her somewhere, stared at each other for a while, and then one of you made a move with small talk.

Today you enjoy the company of your friend and other amazing people because, at some point, you or the other person reached out. But aside from social connections, small talk is an important work skill that is the first step to establishing a relationship with colleagues.

Small talk is a starter for friendly conversations, and there is a proper way to go about it. A significant reason why some people shy away from small talk is that they don't use the appropriate method. Now don't worry if you previously fumbled, you are learning anew, and you will become excellent at it, so continue reading.

One thing's for certain, many of your friendships would not have succeeded had your small talk gone awry. The enemy of small talk is the awkward silence that follows when something goes wrong, such as bringing up a controversial topic. In other words, we must extend our definition of small talk by telling you what does *not* constitute small talk.

To succeed at small talk, you must become familiar with what is expected of you to say and what isn't. I am not saying you will have to memorize the ideas. This is not an exam. Instead, you should become familiar with small talk etiquette, practice intentionally, and it will come naturally to you when you converse.

Small Talk Mistakes to Avoid

Let's look at some of the small talk mistakes you need to avoid when making conversation.

Asking Locational Questions Beyond Where the Conversation Is Taking Place

Remember that the small talk is probably happening at an event or someplace new. You just met this person, and you shouldn't be going beyond your boundaries by talking to them about another place. For example, if you pick up your child from school and run into another parent while making small talk, keep the locational aspects of the conversation to the school setting.

You might run into that parent again or meet him/her somewhere else; then, you can broaden the scope of the conversation. The idea of small talk is to establish friendship without the pressures of divulging extensive information.

If you are talking to someone else for the first time in the office, try to keep all conversations about locations to the office space. When you take this initiative, you will be able to avoid awkward pauses and remain in control of the talk.

Discussing How Much People Make at Work

Within the office setting, people are always curious about how much money their colleagues make. So, some people try to get information from others through small talks by asking indirectly.

Don't do it! At least, don't do this in a culture, such as American culture, where this is not an acceptable norm. This information can be personal. Avoid it until the friendship is better established. Even if the subject of pay comes up, do not segue into a personal question about another's salary.

Offering Unsolicited Advice

This mistake often happens after the person you speak to says something, and you provide some advice or suggestions without their asking.

For example, if the person compliments your look by saying you look fit and healthy, don't then suggest that the person registers at your gym because you feel he/she is obese. This example captures the essence of not offering unusual (and, in some cases, rude) suggestions.

If you do get a compliment during small talk, accept it gracefully and move on to the next idea. If the person requests your advice, then you can offer it, but, even then, it should be polite and straight to the point.

Continuing with a Line of Conversation When the Other Person Isn't Interested

We all have that friend who can talk on and on about a topic even when we are not involved. This trait also tends to affect the flow of small talk.

If the person you are conversing with isn't interested in the topic anymore, move on to a new topic, or end the conversation! So, how will you know when to stop a line of conversation?

You will know from the person's responses, if the person was enthusiastic when talking about the coffee served and loses that enthusiasm when the issue of office furniture crops up, then that's the sign that he/she doesn't want to talk about office furniture. Read the room. If suddenly a person cannot offer so much as a nod, and you meet awkward silence, it's time to talk about something new.

Not Taking the Cue That the Conversation Is About to End

As you would discover in the small sample talk we will consider later, a significant mistake people make with small talk is not getting the cue that the other person wants the conversation to end. If a person's too busy, for instance, or has somewhere they need to be, often they'll hint as much by tapping their foot, looking at the time, or edging toward the nearest doorway.

In a later chapter, we will discuss body language and non-verbal communication. Before we get there, you should know that when the person wants to end the conversation, he/she will give a cue, and you must finish the conversation at that point.

Giving Your Opinion About Controversial Topics Is Not Ideal

Giving your opinion on controversial topics can be a double-edged sword. If you and the person you're talking to happen to share similar views, controversial topics can be a fast-track to a friendship. However, if the coin lands on the other side and the person has opposing views, you might generate animosity or argument. It's best to avoid controversial topics, such as politics, if you don't know how the other person feels.

If someone else presses a controversial topic, find a way to carefully steer the conversation to a safer topic. This way, you don't give the wrong impression.

Giving or Asking About Private Information from a Person

Private information about your life or the person's life is not ideal for small talk. Especially if you're talking with them for the first time, do you think he/she will be enthusiastic about sharing private (sensitive) information with you?

Just as you are not advised to share such information, don't put the other person in a weird position by asking. We are talking about small conversations! It isn't an interrogation or a way to get secrets from a person, so remember the K.I.S.S principle here: *Keep It Short & Simple.*

To emphasize all we have discussed thus far, here is an example below of small talk between two people in an office setting.

Please pay close attention to the *flow* of words and observe how they both communicate; we will discuss what was appropriate and inappropriate in the discussion using the example.

After identifying the mistakes together, I will then show you the better way through which this conversation would have played out.

Sample

Woman: Hi, there.

Man: Hi. I haven't seen you around here. Have you been working for an extended period?

Woman: No, I've been here a few months. I work in the Human Resources section.

Man: You must make more money than I do. I'm in Sales.

Woman: Sale is an exciting job.

Man: It's okay. Hey, you look like you could have a coffee.

Woman: Yes, it's been a hectic week.

Man: Tell me about it! At least it is supposed to be a lovely weekend.

Woman: Yes, I heard they are calling blue skies.

Man: Say, did you watch the game last night?

Woman: No, I was working late.

Man: It was a good game. We won.

Woman: I don't even know who was playing. I'm not a sports fan.

Man: The Chiefs! Do you think they will make it to the finals?

Woman: I'm not sure. I will get back to my desk now.

Man: Speaking of desks, what are your thoughts on the office furniture?

Woman: It's beautiful, but I would instead get paid for my overtime hours.

Man: I think I'll be heading home early. Just in case it snows.

Woman: I know. I can't believe the cold weather. Hopefully, it will be springtime soon.

Man: I can't wait for springtime.

Woman: Me neither! My divorce will finally come through!

Notice much of that conversation felt forced or uncomfortable. Did you find some of the mistakes we discussed earlier? If you didn't, you could reread the small sample talk to try and analyze it for such errors. We will do that together now as well:

- The man said, "You must make more money than I do then," which is wrong for small talk because we are not supposed to talk about what people make in the office.

- Another mistake was when the man asked about the Chiefs and finals. Here, he continued with the subject even when the woman was no longer interested.

- Did you observe when the man kept talking about the "desks?" he didn't take the cue that the woman wanted the conversation to end.

- The woman also committed a small talk blunder by mentioning, "Getting paid for overtime hours." She gave her opinion on a controversial subject, which is inappropriate.

- The woman mentioned her divorce. A divorce is private and sensitive information that shouldn't be shared during small talk.

We have identified the mistakes and analyzed the errors, well done! Now I want to show you the exact small talk scenario with this sample. This corrected version will help you appreciate the value of little talks when done right and how you can ace it every time.

Corrected Sample

Woman: Hi there.

Man: I haven't seen you around here before. Have you worked here long?

Woman: No, I've only been here for a few months. I work in the human resources department.

Man: Oh, that must be why I haven't seen you around. I'm in sales.

Woman: Sales sounds like an exciting job.

Man: It's okay. I could use coffee; it's been a hectic week.

Woman: Yes, it's been a hectic week for me, too.

Man: Tell me about it! At least it's supposed to be a lovely weekend.

Woman: Yes, I've heard that they are calling for blue skies.

Man: Say, did you watch the game last night?

Woman: No, I was working late.

Man: I think I'll be heading home early today. It might snow. I better get going. See you tomorrow!

Woman: See you![1]

This chapter is a foundational one that has introduced you to the basic idea of small talk. Everything we will learn or discover in subsequent chapters will be linked to this section, so keep all we've discussed in mind.

There are challenges with the idea of small talk! Some of these challenges are caused by the personality and behavioral traits of the individual. In the next chapter, you will find two such issues and learn how to overcome them.

---

[1]*Excerpts from small sample talk was derived from English Club.com. Please see the reference list for a direct link.

CHAPTER TWO

Overcoming Fear and Shyness

A lot of us are very afraid to make small talks, especially the introverts who worry too much and think it will be awkward, boring, or maybe they will run out of what to say when they initiate the conversation. However, with the evolution of the world and with the way the world is now based on mostly connections, avoiding small talk is like avoiding seeing people; it is very difficult, people are everywhere, and you will surely see them and make conversations. Networking events, parties, or having lunch at work will always provide opportunities to meet people and exchange pleasantries.

You will get to understand that making small talk isn't as painful as it seems. Once you learn to overcome the obstacles surrounding you making it, you will be able to polish your skills and make a better impression.

Fear and shyness make some people feel inadequate when making small talk. In this chapter, we are going to start practicing how to execute excellent small talk by first getting rid of specific challenges, such as fear and shyness. Here, you will discover the importance of confidence, how to turn anxiety into excitement, and how you can focus on the present. Get ready to dive into a bit of stoicism as you learn how to discover yourself.

Fear in a person when he/she converses with another person means confidence is absent. This realization should propel you to want to build self-confidence as a necessary skill for executing successful small talk. We will talk about confidence a lot because it is a deal-breaker, but why is it so crucial?

Why Is Confidence Important?

Your confidence level influences your thoughts, which means that it can either boost the success of your small talk or defeat it. If you are less confident about approaching someone for small talk, if you are afraid of doing it, you will end up being boring.

Understand that you are a worthy person with a lot of exciting things to say. Sometimes the root of a lack of confidence lies within a feeling of unworthiness. When we feel like we are not worthy, we tend to feel less confident, and that is where problems begin.

Always keep this in mind: other people in the office or other social functions are just looking for someone to chat with. As such, you must relieve yourself of pressure that compels you to try and "impress" them.

Confidence is knowing that you bring something to the table and sharing your thoughts most articulately. If the person you converse with feels like you are not comfortable or confident, the conversation can end abruptly.

So how can you build such confidence when you make small talk?

Be Interested

To be a confident and attractive person, you must be involved in the person you are talking to and the subjects you both cover. This idea is not only a good step towards building confidence, but it is also crucial in helping you make great small talk. In addition, by showing interest, you feed into the self-confidence of your conversational partner. You may ask, "How can I show interest?" Let your curious side out to play! Maybe you'll learn something new.

Be Relatable

It is also crucial that you don't monopolize the conversation, which means you need to attempt being relatable. The other person shouldn't just feel led on in the conversation but feel like a part of it and that they can relate to what you're saying.

If the person mentions that they like being fit, you can add that you agree on the role that exercise plays in good health (or something like that). Inject your observations, share relatable experiences, and be calm.

Ask Questions

You don't have to ask deep-rooted questions that will require a lot of thinking. Ask simple questions, "How was your week?" "Are you enjoying the event?" and then listen for the answer. Don't ask questions because you feel compelled to without paying attention to the response.

To keep the flow of conversation going, you can also ask follow-up questions, which shows that you are listening to the person. If the person says they are not enjoying the event, for example, you may give a little chuckle to lighten the mood and ask why.

Be Present

You will show a higher level of confidence while conversing when you are 100% present. A smile wouldn't hurt, uncross your arms, and avoid looking over your shoulder (it makes it seem like you are bored and you want to leave).

More importantly, when making small talk, keep your hands off your smartphone or mobile devices.

Use the Twenty Seconds Rule

Dr. Mark Goulston, a clinical psychiatrist and communications expert, inspired the twenty seconds rule, and it is crucial for successful small talks. Dr. Goulston recommends that when speaking, the other person will only be interested in what you say during the first twenty seconds.

Beyond that, the other person starts to lose interest. In addition, the other might mistake you for self-absorbed. Practice the rule to mastery.

Turn Anxiety into Excitement

Think of anxiety and fear as two sides of the same coin. With that coin, you might be tempted to flip it or leave it up to chance. Let's try a different strategy, however. You choose which side is face up.

When you are anxious or excited, your heart beats faster; you experience rapid breathing, mild trembling, sweaty palms, and an unusual tensed feeling. You also feel nervous, unfocused, and sometimes sleeplessness.

There are similarities between the symptoms of anxiety and those of excitement, so why not turn one (which is negative) to the other (which is positive)? Whenever you feel anxious, have a pep talk with yourself and get excited, let this be your reflex action whenever you feel uneasy.

Yes, it is possible to train yourself to always turn anxiety into excitement, and it is easier than you think. Until now, the goal has been to remain calm, i.e. to suppress anxiety. Rather, it might serve better to take all that energy and turn it into something more productive.

How do you do that? I want this process to be as smooth and natural to you. That's why I created an easy step-by-step guide.

Step One: Embrace Your Emotions

Don't try to fight off the anxious spells you feel, if you are nervous, allow yourself to handle it. Yes, it will be uncomfortable, but you've got to endure it and become aware of the sensations you feel. How do you feel? Are you restless? Trembling? Sweating? Embrace all these emotions, and they will not overwhelm you.

Step Two: Stop Beating Yourself Up

Next, stop beating yourself. If you allow self-sabotaging thoughts to obstruct you, you will under-perform. You might have noticed in times of success, during a presentation, for example, you never exactly stopped being nervous. Instead, you stopped telling yourself "*I can't*," and you just *did.*

19

Step Three: Tell Yourself to Get Excited

At this stage, you need to reframe your emotions by telling yourself to get excited. Acknowledge the feeling of excitement and *not* anxiety (this is where you choose). If you do as much, convincing yourself that you're excited, then you will be.

Step Four: Visualize a Successful Small Talk

The role of visualization is crucial! Imagine yourself doing what you are about to do impressively. Always inject details of the conversation you can see, hear, and feel in your imagination.

Most of the time, you will get what you replay in your imagination. If you envision a failed conversation, then you will fail at it. If you envision a successful small talk, you will get that—if your expectations are reasonable, of course.

Focus on the Present

The present is fleeting, hence the expression "no time like the present", which is why you must make the most out of it. Confidence will make you seize the present and not try to envision what could happen in the future.

This sounds contrary to advice about visualization, and, in some sense, it is. You're visualizing something that may or may not happen in the future. However, the point of remaining present isn't to forget about the future—after all, your goal is successful small talk. Rather, the point is that, in the moments that count, you're no longer daydreaming. You're there. You're present.

20

That conversational moment is what counts, so stop anticipating what could go wrong. Stop thinking if you will stutter, say the wrong thing, or do something with a terrible future implication.

Destructive thoughts serve only one purpose, which is to disorientate you and cause self-doubt.

Let's enjoy a little imaginative/mindfulness exercise, shall we? At this moment, imagine that there is no future, and there is no past, only the present moment. Forget about the experiences you had in the past, school, home, childhood, university, etc. and focus on the now.

How do you feel? Do you feel constrained when you have no past worries? Do you still feel pressure when you have nothing to worry about in the future? Now relax and connect to the present moment, and only focus on yourself alone.

Tell me. What do you feel? The answers will vary, but one thing is for sure, you will definitely be your most authentic self. You would say whatever you want to say and do whatever you want to do; you will be free! There will be no future consequence nor past regrets, and you won't have to bother about making great first impressions either.

Now the exercise above represents an imaginative utopia, but I had to express it to you so you can imagine the extent of freedom you will enjoy when you focus on the present. People who are shy often overthink and worry about what people will say about them afterward.

You need to set all these worries aside and be free, confident, and assured in the fact that you will do well. Don't forget that you may not get another opportunity to have that "small talk" with the same person again. When you meet him/her in the future, it will be a continuation of the first talk, and it inevitably wouldn't be tagged small talk again.

So, I'm telling you to relax and take it all one step at a time. Focus on executing the small talk at the office before thinking about the wedding ceremony you need to attend next week.

Take it all in one at a time, and you will do great. (One great way to put the above exercise to use is by practicing mindfulness meditation).

Know Thyself

Yep, time for some philosophy. One way to know one's self is through a philosophy called Stoicism. First developed in ancient Greece c. 300 B.C.E., the well-known Roman emperor Marcus Aurelius' adoption of the principles likely contributes to the popularity stoicism enjoys even today and the shift from more theoretical to practical applications of the philosophy.

Modern Stoicism teaches that virtue is happiness and our judgment should be based on behavior instead of words. This idea teaches us that we can only rely on ourselves and not on external events. This means that, when relating to someone else through small talk, you must understand that you cannot control the other person's narrative, you can only control yours. Modern Stoicism is a tool we can use to be better individuals who excel at our jobs, relationships, and even while communicating with strangers because we are aware of the power in knowing ourselves.

Stoicism encourages a meditative process that allows you to take negative feelings and turn them into thoughts that give you peace and a better perspective on life. This philosophical idea helps you develop a better mindset and enables you to look inward by asking yourself questions about life. So how do all these ideas translate into you knowing yourself?

Well, when you spend so much time looking inwards and getting answers to the situations you find you will be honest with yourself. You will get to know how you think, the aspects to work on, and how you can relate on a better level with others (especially through small talk).

To know yourself, you need to ascertain the kind of social environment where you thrive. Yes, it is crucial to be able to adapt to any social situation, but it is essential for you to know yourself and know where you are most comfortable.

Stoicism will help you become better at knowing yourself, and in that state, regardless of your character type (introverted or extroverted), you will see the kind of situations you enjoy. For example, when you start practicing your small talk, avoid using locations you are not comfortable in, and stick to the ones that come naturally to you.

What do you know about yourself? Do you like intimate gatherings? Large parties? Are you a very extroverted person? These are questions I cannot answer for you, and there are the questions that will lead the way in helping find yourself.

If you loathe large gatherings, then you would have a more difficult time with small talk. On the other hand, if you love smaller crowds, you will probably talk to almost everyone in the room before the party ends.

You can see that the dynamics of small talk changes based on who you are and your preferences. An introverted person will want to practice more privately before getting on the scene.

Philosophy may be a tool to help, but, in reality, there is no universal manual for socializing. Remember, perfection is the enemy of the good, as Voltaire said. Do what works best for you and maintain your flow while getting better. What stoicism can do is help you become excited about what you do because you know yourself. You know what you can do and ready to take on any situation.

When you meet a person who isn't self-aware or confident, you'll see that their conversations do not reflect their complete personality because they are unsure of themselves. I don't want you to read this book and try to implement small talk while being unsure of yourself.

Practice stoicism, be mindful, and enjoy the process of getting to know yourself.

What Is in Keeping with Your Character?

The concept of rationality and irrationality varies from person to person, and this applies to the idea of good and evil. This realization expresses a significant reason why we need to learn how to adjust any preconceived notions we may have about these ideals.

We must understand that what might be useful to you might be viewed as bad to someone else. If you meet that "someone" who sees your good as evil, will you change it for them? Can you stay true to your character despite the differences in opinions that occur in the world?

To be successful at small talk while fighting off fear and anxiety, you must keep in touch with character. The world is very diverse, and it is easy for anyone to lose their identity, especially when they don't know their character.

While at a social event, it will be much easier for you to allow irrational fears, and your opinions get to you. You will feel like you are following an invisible script, patterns, and instructions because you are under pressure to conform and maintain a specific social skill code.

But the more you get to know who you are, the easier it will be for you to become your compass. You will value your convictions and thoughts, holding them in high regard because they are yours. You will be comfortable sharing your ideas because you know such thoughts belong to no one else.

Character is powerful!

Your character is a tool that enables you to internally seek out what you believe in and know your interests because these are the distinguishing factors that set you aside from others. Since small talks are all about making authentic connections, you will need to trust yourself, hence why you must also know yourself. Your words and actions should reflect who you are.

When you initiate discussions, do you feel like yourself? Or do you feel pressure to speak in a certain way that will be pleasing to the other person? Do you change your opinions easily because you want to conform to another person's idea?

Your experiences with small talk will be a whole lot easier when you stay true to who you are and your character. You will also avoid toxic relationships, the wrong people, poisonous jobs, fair-weathered friends (they drain so much energy), and other ills that affect people who do not know their character.

Please note that this realization with character doesn't mean you have to embark on a journey of self-discovery. I am merely imploring you to ask yourself questions that will inspire a sense of awareness within you.

All forms of conversations are linked to connections, but the purpose of connecting with others will be lost if you don't hold on to who you are now. The people you interact with will meet a "different you" all the time because you have an inconsistent character.

Do you remember when you went for your first date? You were probably giddy with excitement while anticipating meeting your date. The reason for the anticipation is because you couldn't wait to learn more about this person.

Just as you anticipated spending time with a total stranger, you need to spend time with yourself. When you spend time with yourself, you will be able to align your interests and get to know the true nature of your character. Knowing your personality will, in turn, sharpen your level of confidence, eliminate fear, and allow you to enjoy the process of connecting with others.

Fear and anxiety only cripple those who lose themselves to others, what can you do to fix this? Take yourself out on dates, know who you are focused on the present, and turn your anxiety to excitement.

This process of self-discovery, dispelling of fear, and mastery of confidence is an important part of small talk. We're making progress! In the next section, you will learn all about the social code and how it relates to making small talk.

CHAPTER THREE

Non-Verbal Communication and the Social Code

Anxiety and fear-free people, as discussed in Chapter 2, will have no difficulty with this section. Here, you will learn all about the concept of a social skills code, which is closely related to the four sides model, also known as the communication square or four ears model.

This chapter will help you avoid misunderstandings. The concepts in this chapter will show you how to speak coherently and succeed at all small talk.

Let's look at a communication model developed by German psychologist Friedemann Schulz von Thun, an expert on interpersonal and intrapersonal communication. Based on his model, every message has four essential parts that are not the same but must be individually considered. The four aspects of the message include factual information, appeal, relationship, and self-revelation.

So, what's important about it in terms of small talk? Simple. Learning more about the nature of communication will make you better at it. The better you are at communication, the fewer misunderstandings you'll have.

To understand the four-side model well enough, we must start with the two people involved and the message component:

1. Sender

The sender is the individual who delivers the message; this is the person that says something. So, if you were conversing with someone else, the time you spoke, you would be the sender.

2. Receiver

The receiver receives the message; this person listens to the sender.

3. Message

The other component is the message. These are the actual contents of what each sender says: the words and the tone.

When you engage in small talk, all three components will be present, but whether or not you're able to avoid misunderstandings depends on your ability to process all three components at the same time. Many misunderstandings come from a receiver only paying attention to one component without considering the others.

The four sides of communication introduced earlier help you see everything during small talk. Let's analyze each level:

The Factual Information Level

The first level of communication in the four sides model is the factual level. As the name of the level suggests, it's about the exchanged facts during communication: objective data devoid of subjective inputs. For example, if I say, "the laptop is $599.99," that's matter-of-fact. It's simply data.

However, factual information isn't always communicated matter-of-factly. Sometimes the receiver infers fact. Much of the information that's misunderstood is implicit, remember. Take this sentence as an example: "It took me a long time to get here. The drive was difficult." This might be interpreted as "traffic is bad." Is it? Is that what was said? Not necessarily. Even at the factual level, misunderstandings can happen.

The Self-revealing or Self-disclosure Level

During communication, the self-revealing level is information about the sender that's implicitly revealed (or at least thought to be revealed). If, for instance, I say, "Why do you even like sour cream"? You might infer that I don't like sour cream because I've asked you with incredulity.

But it's important to keep in mind that this is an inference. It may or may not be true. It's distinct from the factual level of the four sides model because it's not a fact but rather a conjecture.

The Relationship Level

When analyzing small talk, sometimes you'll find information revealed about the relationship between the sender and the receiver (or yourself and another). When a sender talks to the receiver, something they say might send a cue to the receiver that the sender feels a specific

31

way about them. In other words, at the relationship level, the receiver determines: "He/she thinks *this/that* about me."

This is yet another inference based on implicit rather than explicit information. If I say, "What are you doing here?" to a friend who showed up unexpected or uninvited to a party, they could interpret that as "He doesn't like me. We're not good friends." Again, that's not necessarily proven or disproven.

The Appeal Level

At the appeal level, the receiver is trying to determine: "What do they (the sender) want?". Here's an example. Your boss says, "If we had these reports earlier, we could have reacted more appropriately." You could interpret this as the boss saying: "Don't be late on reports."

Each of the levels above can be misinterpreted individually between the sender and receiver, the intent of the message can be different, the same with their meaning. When people understand things differently, they also tend to react/respond differently, as well.

Below is an example of how the four sides of this communication style work:

Two people meet at the buffet stand during a party, one of them is the caterer, and the other is a guest.

Sender: "This pasta has proteins."

The potential intention of the sender based on the four levels is as follows:

Factual level: There is protein in the pasta.

Appeal level: Tell me what kind of protein!

Relationship level: You should know what kind of protein

Self-revealing level: I don't like proteins in my pasta.

Receiver's perception/perceived intent through analysis (remember that the receiver is the caterer here)

Factual level: There is protein in the pasta.

Appeal level: I can't cook what you like because it is a party.

Relationship level: Are you questioning my cooking?

Self-revealing level: You don't know what the protein is that makes you feel uncomfortable.

This pasta example shows just how easy it is for misunderstanding to occur between the sender and receiver. There is always the massive potential for misunderstanding during small talk, hence, the reason you need to know how to relate in a way that all levels are in-sync for clarity.

The sender always has an intention that is hidden/implicit in the message. The purpose of the word is what he/she wants to convey. The receiver, on the other hand, analyzes the information heard by matching it against his/her beliefs, experiences, and values. So, think of the process this way:

Sender: Intention = Truth

Receiver: Perception = Truth

Sender's Truth = Receiver's Truth

Please note that the receiver's truth may not be the sender's truth. This process happens so fast, and most of it is subconscious. Some people have a default channel through which they send and receive messages due to past experiences, their belief systems, etc.

To avoid misunderstanding, you must know how to use the four-side model effectively when making small talk. Again, the only way you can make this work is through intentional and persistent practice. How can you start practicing to get better?

Below I'll show you how best to manage a small talk situation from both sides (as sender and receiver). You can practice with both ideas until you get it right.

Begin with the first phase of communication: *thinking*. If you are the sender, please think about what you want to say and your intention for saying it. What information do you want to send? If you are a receiver, listen for the exact information your partner is communicating and how else you can understand the message.

Next, as a sender, you've got to ensure that your intentions are explicit and not vague. Ask what the receiver heard and what they make of the conversation before saying something new.

If you are the receiver, ask if you understood what was said, you could say something along the lines of: "Do you mean...?" or "To clarify, do you mean ..."

This exercise can be done repeatedly for all four sides of communication, and then you will be excited at the fact that all your messages are received without any misunderstanding. Through practice, you can make progress with using this model.

Understanding is crucial for the success of small talks, and it begins with knowing a lot about the varying aspects of speech, as analyzed in this chapter. Now you know how the four-side model works and how you can appropriate it to your small talk experience.

Can we move on to another exciting idea? I'll assume you that's a resounding "yes!", so let's consider the role of non-verbal communication next. The details of the next chapter take some inspiration from this chapter as non-verbal communication is important when trying to understand others.

CHAPTER FOUR

Using Body Language in Small Talk

Non-verbal communication is as old as man, and it is just as important as verbal communication. But why doesn't it get as much attention as verbal communication? Most likely because we were raised to listen to words and not observe body movement.

This chapter focuses on non-verbal communication as a vital part of making small talk. You will learn how to utilize non-verbal cues and observe peoples' body movements for responses while communicating. Let's get right to it then!

Have you ever said something without "saying" it? Think about it before answering.

If your answer is affirmative, surely you agree that non-verbal communication can be a swifter way of sending a message. Pointing, hand gestures, head tilts, and all the like can help communicate messages, and can even help avoid the misunderstandings discussed in Chapter 3.

According to a study by Professor Mehrabian, communication is 7% verbal and 93% non-verbal. The non-verbal component constitutes body language at 55% and the tone of voice at 38%. This means you can say one thing with your words, but that your body language can send a completely different message.

So, the goal for everyone who wants to excel at making small talk should be to improve their understanding and use of non-verbal signals so they can fully express what they mean without contradiction. If you don't want misunderstandings and want to build stronger relationships, your verbal and non-verbal speech must use the same language.

Due to the nature of the small talk, you may not have the opportunity to correct a misunderstanding by saying, "Oh, this was what I meant". Remember! This is small talk. It's short, sweet, and meant to build relationships. There's little room for error. You have only a few minutes to pass your message across in the best way possible.

If your non-verbal signs agree with your spoken words, this increases clarity, rapport, and trust between you and the other person. When they don't align, it leads to tension, confusion, and mistrust. You need to be very sensitive to these ideas to become a better communicator. More so, your sensitivity has to go beyond the spoken communication to the non-verbal one.

Let's take this instance as an example of the powerful way of nonverbal communication. Imagine your best friend or spouse arrived at your house right before dinner. Her lips were tight, face red, and eyebrows furrowed. She refused to speak to anyone. After pacing back and forth throughout the room, she threw her bag on the couch and plopped down in the chair beside the window. After a few seconds of her glaring out the window, you asked, "Are you OK? I hope all is well?" She yelled, "I'm fine!"

Now, let me ask, which of these messages are you going to believe. Is it her verbal communication, which says she is fine or the nonverbal cues which consist of her tone of voice and behavior? I believe you will most likely believe the nonverbal cues she gave.

Below we will learn what verbal clues entail, specifically about the types for small talk and how you can use body language to succeed with excellent communication. Please note that with some of the ideas you will find below there are cultural implications as well, so I offer some explanations on these implications. We must be respectful to others while communicating.

What Exactly Are Nonverbal Cues?

According to Patti Wood, an author and expert in body language, nonverbal cues constitute most of the communication between people without having a direct translation. These cues can be in the form of nuances of the voice, body movements, body orientation, facial expressions, choice, and the movement of the objects that contributes to communication, and details of the dress. Space and time can also be nonverbal cues.

To simply put, nonverbal cues are how you show, express, and present yourself, and not just the words that come out of your mouth. These nonverbal cues are very important in your business, and at work because "perception is reality".

In communication, our senses play a vital role as all good conscience, credibility, and proof of truth can only come from the senses. How we are being perceived or 'sensed' by other people will greatly impact our success in our businesses or workplace. If this is not the case, a lot of people will be misjudged. People with great ideas, the brilliant ones, and people with exceptional talent will be mislabeled, misjudged, and ignored because of the ineffectiveness of nonverbal cues.

Since nonverbal cues are mostly sent from the "emotional brain" and not the neocortex (also known as isocortex and neopallium). The neocortex is involved in higher functions like generation of motor commands, sensory perception, conscious thought, and spatial reasoning in people. This emotional brain helps to create a more honest answer and revealing messages during conversations.

According to Wood, nonverbal cues enables business owners to determine the motivation of others and analyze business interactions in a depth, better, and richer way than just relying on printed or spoken words.

Wood suggested that people who can understand nonverbal cues can assess what their customers, co-workers, and clients are actually telling them, just to know how to satisfy their needs better. "Employers can evaluate the messages their employees are sending to customers, clients or fellow workers and know whether that employee is hurting or helping business," he says. Employees too can learn to understand those subtle signs that their bosses send; this will help them adjust their behavior when needed.

Effectively using nonverbal communication is vital in your career development. When an employer is looking for a talent to hire, or promoting an existing employee, the traits they normally look for include professionalism, enthusiasm, and confidence. As an employee, to express these and all other leadership traits they might be looking for requires you to send the right nonverbal cues.

Let's dive into the types of nonverbal cues that will help you with small talks.

Types of Non-verbal Cues for Small Talk

Since we can't avoid sending nonverbal cues to people, it is important to train yourself to send the right ones. Below, we will be looking at the types of nonverbal cues that are essential for small talks.

Facial Expression

Did you know that the most expressive part of your body is your face? Oh yes, it is, and it is the first observable feature the person you talk to notices even before you start talking.

You can say a lot with your face, even more than your words. Have you ever spoken to someone before, and they had frown lines across their forehead? It might have felt disrespectful even if the person didn't intend to be rude.

You can convey countless emotions without saying a word, and unlike other forms of non-verbal communication, facial expressions are universal. A person smiling in China and a person smiling in America is usually the same message despite the differences in location. Of course, there are different types of smiles: some sinister, some greeting, some mirthful, some questioning—but research supports that the lines that create these expressions in our faces are more or less the same in spite of culture.

Across all cultures, facial expressions are the same. We express happiness, surprise, fear, and disgust in almost the same way, which shows the impact of this non-verbal cue. While building your level of confidence and getting rid of fear, also make sure you pay attention to your facial expressions. If you are saying something pleasant, what should you be doing? You should be smiling! If you are considering an idea, you should tilt your head like you are thinking about it. Small talk will go exceptionally well when your facial expressions are in agreement with your words.

Tone of Voice

With the sound of the voice, you should know that it isn't solely about what you say, but *how* you say it. When you speak, the other person gets your voice in addition to your words, and your voice can mean something different from your words.

The words, "sit down" and "sit down!" are the same words but the exclamation produces a different tone. An exclamation usually implies increased volume or increased enthusiasm.

The timing and pace also matter. Faster speech usually implies urgency (or perhaps anxiety) whereas slower speech usually communicates calmness. In such ways, your voice can express affection, confidence, sarcasm, and much more. The sound of your voice can be overlooked when discussing non-verbal communicative cues because people merge it with speaking, but it doesn't entail words, so it is non-verbal. Learn how to fluctuate your tone of voice appropriately to achieve exciting small talk experiences.

Eye Contact

The way you look at someone communicates a lot about you to them, and it is one of the most crucial non-verbal communication cues. Your eyes can express affection, hostility, attraction, interests, tiredness, etc.

If you want to maintain the flow of small talk and enjoy the process, you must pay close attention to how you use eye contact. We will extensively discuss how to make good eye contact in the next section of this chapter: How to Use Body Language When Making Small Talk.

The way you carry yourself is a reflection of who you are and how you want people to relate to you. You also communicate with how you sit, walk, stand, or hold your head, which is why posture is crucial here. Your posture should reflect how you feel, and for a good first impression during small talk, it should exude confidence.

Gestures

Gestures are a part of our daily experiences. You might have even gestured while reading this book (without knowing it). Gestures are done with the hands, and there are varying types: waving, beckoning, pointing, or using your hands while speaking or arguing.

When you raise your hands to your face level a little bit while speaking, it means you are trying to make a crucial point. When you run your hands through your hair while speaking, it could mean that you are nervous or unsure. If you point, then you are trying to make the person see what you are talking about.

You should know that gestures have varying meanings per culture. The "Ok" sign made with the hand, for example, conveys a message of positivity in most English-speaking countries. But in some countries, such as France, Venezuela, Turkey, and Brazil, it's offensive.

Of course, you wouldn't know all the offensive gestures based on all cultures, but you can take a cue from the person.

Touch

We also communicate a great deal through touch because human connections also happen through contact. If two people gave you a handshake, for example, with one being weak and one being firm, you would most likely remember the one who gave a firm handshake more than the other one with a weak handshake.

What about hugs? If you are allowed to give hugs at that first meeting, you can give a bear hug and make the person feel more comfortable around you (or perhaps more uncomfortable in cultures for whom personal space is of higher value). In some other cases, you will be required to provide a pat on the back or a mild grip on the arm.

Be mindful of how you use this non-verbal style because you don't want to be too touchy with the person. In some cultures, touch while making small talk may be inappropriate, and then sometimes the occasion might not be one where you need to be touchy. This is especially true of communication between people of the opposite sex.

With this non-verbal communicative style, you need to apply a lot of tact and caution. But if you sense that you can use touch, be generous but careful with it.

How to Use Body Language When Making Small Talk

While growing up, I was in a rush to make friends. After some trial and error, I realized that making friends, building lasting friendships, and connecting with people takes time. Before you connect with people, you need to get to know them. Now I kick myself after realizing that most of the time I'd been forcing connections by inviting myself to parties or having conversations people didn't really want to have with me.

Building lasting friendships doesn't take a day, it is a gradual process that often starts with a simple smile or hello. Some of the steps needed can be harder than others, but you should feel comfortable when you use your body language to attract people and make small talk with people! Let's look at how to use our body language when making small talk.

Don't Cross Your Arms or Legs

Crossing your arms or legs while speaking is not ideal for fruitful discussions. When you cross your arms, you appear defensive, and you also look uncomfortable, which might prompt the other person to end the conversation.

Instead of crossing your arms, use them to gesture. Instead of crossing legs, maintain an open stance that communicates welcomeness (unless you're wearing a skirt). The idea is mostly to remain relaxed and comfortable.

Make Eye Contact, But Don't Stare

The eyes are essential when talking about non-verbal communication because we can say a lot with them. What you shouldn't do, however, is to stare at the person, making eye contact isn't the same as staring.

Staring can be considered offensive by some people, so refrain from doing that. When saying something to the person or replying to a question, you can look him/her in the eye. But also move your eyes around the person's face and occasionally around the room.

Making eye contact shows your level of confidence, and it also informs the other person that you are present during the brief yet impactful conversation. Don't worry about executing all these cues flawlessly; remain aware, and you will do just fine!

Relax Your Shoulders

You may not know this, but your shoulders speak loudly, and you've got to keep them in check. A tensed shoulder is a non-verbal sign that you want to leave the room, and you are done talking. While a relaxed shoulder is a signal that you are ready to enjoy the conversation.

An excellent way to relax your shoulders is to take deep breaths before approaching the individual because one of the reasons for a stiff shoulder is anxiety. You may not even know that your joints are stiff, but the other person can see it, so be mindful of it. Here is a tip, you will know that your shoulders are tensed when you feel the tension on your collarbone and neck region, whenever you feel that pressure, know that your shoulders are tensed and loosen up.

Nod

How do you feel when talking to someone else, and they nod in acknowledgment? A nod tells the other that you're listening. It's an effective tool to show that you're present and remain respectful to your small talk partner.

Sit up Straight (Don't Slouch)

If you are discussing with someone and you both get to sit, don't slouch. Slouching signals that you are tired, disinterested, or want to go home.

Sit up straight like the confident person that you are and share your thoughts most concisely. When you don't slouch, you also get to pay close attention to the other person and minimize distractions.

Lean In!

When we say "lean in," we are referring to your ability to tear down the walls that may affect the proper connection between you and the other person. When a person meets you for the first time, within the opening seconds, they try to figure you out.

Leaning in is a way to drop your guard and signal we're available and present.

Ensure that you are a good listener who understands the meaning of what you are hearing. Keep your eyes on the person (but don't stare) while nodding as you listen. But always be aware of personal space. Leaning in too much, as former president Lyndon B. Johnson was known for with his so-called Treatment, can also be intimidating and overbearing.

Smile and Laugh (When Appropriate)

There are moments during the conversation when you should smile and laugh, comply with this step as it would help you maintain a positive flow of communication. Small talk is what it is, so there is no need for you to be all stiff.

If you sense a stiffness with the other person, try to create some ease by smiling, say something a little funny that gives way for a laugh.

Mirror Body Language

The essence of mirroring in communication is to improve the rapport between both parties. What you do here is to imitate the person's physical mannerisms and positions to bond with them.

Sometimes we practice mirroring without being conscious of it. Yawn! If you suddenly felt like yawning just from seeing the word, that's unplanned mirroring.

When conversing with a person and they smile, you can mirror their body language by smiling back at them. By doing this, you are keeping the flow of the conversation and maintaining a great connection with them.

When two people mirror each other, it shows comfort and trust. Mirroring works most smoothly when you've known the person for a long time; for example, romantic couples can easily mirror each other. But with small talk, you are probably talking to this person for the first time. As such, you will have to pay closer attention to them. You must observe them and then reply with non-verbal communication through mirroring.

So, if the other person smiles, please take it as a cue from them and smile back. If they appear to relax and you feel tensed, mirror their calm by being rested as well. Mirrors are mostly a non-verbal idea and something you can achieve by being present during the conversation. For you to become great at mirroring, you need to practice a lot with all your interactions and pay attention to others.

But the bulk of the work doesn't rest solely on you as the other person will also mirror you. You can ensure that you portray whatever you want the other person to reflect. Do you want them relaxed and calm? Then smile more often while injecting little laughs here and there.

If they take your cue and mirror you, the talk will move smoothly.

Respect Personal Space

Lastly, please respect the other person's own space. We are all different, but we will all agree that we love it when people appreciate our space. If you don't respect people's areas, you will make a wrong first impression that will affect follow-up conversation.

As you speak with this individual, try to maintain a reasonable distance, and don't initiate personal touches if you are unsure of how the person will react. For example, don't give unwarranted hugs, high fives, or touch their bodies.

You've just met this person, and you don't know their orientation about such things. It will be better for you both if he/she initiates it, then you will be on the safer side.

How Non-Verbal Communication Can Go Wrong with Small Talk in an Office (or Anywhere Else).

Within the office space or anywhere you go to regularly, people form impressions of others based on non-verbal communication.

A person may be intentionally trying to be great at small talk with all the "right" words and fail at it because of a lack of excellent non-verbal communication. Now, people avoid speaking with the person because his/her non-verbal skills are sending the wrong message.

We will analyze three personalities with great intentions for successful small talk with others. However, they struggle in their attempt to connect with others, and they are not aware of the wrong non-verbal message they communicate.

Meet Andrea, Meghan, and John!

Andrea

Andrea looks excellent, and she's a good conversationalist but is also very distracted. She claims to be great at speaking, but when talking with someone, her eyes dart all around the room, thus giving the impression that she isn't present.

The people that Andrea talks to feel ignored after the first few seconds of meeting her. They think she is self-absorbed, even though she feels like she is excellent at communicating.

Andrea needs to learn how to strike a balance between her impressive speaking ability and how she uses her eyes to communicate as well.

Meghan

Meghan is a beautiful lady who wants to connect with eligible men (in the office and other social events). But she always has a difficult time maintaining small talk, even though she thinks she's funny and exciting.

Despite her constant laughs and smiles, Meghan's voice is raised, and her body is stiff. When great guys are around her, they feel anxious and uncomfortable, so they quickly cut the conversation short, leaving Meghan confused.

Even though Meghan has got jokes, her body language says something else, and this will consistently be a hindrance to everything she tries to achieve with small talk.

John

John believes that he gets along well with his colleagues, especially the new employees he has had small talks with. But if you ask some of these new employees and his other colleagues, they will all agree that he is "tense" which makes it challenging to enjoy chatting with him.

Some of his colleagues claim that he doesn't just look at a person, he stares for a long time, and with handshakes, he squeezes too hard (it hurts). John, on the other hand, believes that he is trying to show interest in people, hence the reason he makes eye contact for too long.

Despite his efforts, his non-verbal signals make him appear awkward and keep people at a distance. John will struggle with making progress with communication at work because he is not aware of this non-verbal challenge. He is a lesson in moderation.

The examples above show the willingness of the individuals to communicate effectively (they've got good intentions). But they struggle because they lack awareness of how best to utilize non-verbal signals. With the tips provided above, you can make the most out of every moment mixing great verbal and non-verbal communication skills.

Non-verbal communication is always a fascinating topic, especially within the confines of small talk. People speak all the time using non-verbal cues consciously or unconsciously, what matters is if you are paying attention to what they are saying.

You can also communicate with someone else through non-verbal communication, and this chapter has expressed all of that. We are adding more layers to our learning experience; it has been exciting, coming from the basic ideas in section one to where we are now. But we are not done yet as there are still so many ideas to uncover. In the next chapter, we'll finally discuss what comes after hello.

CHAPTER FIVE

After Hello, Breaking the Ice

Saying hello to someone in a social setting or the office seems easy. Think about it. Anyone can say hello and move on. However, the aim of small talk isn't just to move on afterward. You will need to lay the foundation for a follow-up conversation with the person. Now, this is where the challenge begins for a lot of people that struggle with small talk; they wonder, "What should I say after hello?"

This chapter will teach you how to hold an exciting and memorable conversation after saying hello. You will learn the essential qualities of the best conversation starters. You will also discover how to make a good first impression.

Generally, what comes after hello is referred to as a conversation starter, which entails the things you say to the person that kick-starts the small talk properly. As easy as it may sound, some people get stuck because quite frankly, the number of things that can be said is practically infinite. Still, the question is, which is most appropriate?

Remember that small talk aims to strike a connection with another and not just to talk excessively on nothing in particular. You've got to speak in such a graceful and concise manner that you can pick up the conversation with the person again another time, and it will flow naturally.

But please note that the tips for conversation starters I'll provide are not exclusive. They're not the only things you can or should say. This book is training you, but more importantly, the best way to learn practically about small talk is by, well, talking. So, don't worry! While the ideas here aim to sharpen your skills, sometimes you have to go with the flow and say what comes to mind.

For you to achieve a profound connection after saying hello, you've got to know some of the qualities of good conversation starters. These qualities are a guide on what the content of your conversation starter should be, but don't worry. I will elaborate on them with an example, so you know how to apply them to your particular small talk situation.

Four Qualities of the Best Conversation Starters

1. Great Starters Deliver Confidently

The best starters are the ones you deliver in a self-assured way, making it easier for the other person to join in on the conversation. Confidence is likened to a magnet when you exude it; others catch on and are attracted to it. Confidence is one of the best qualities you need to speak to others from the start.

For example, when you walk up to a person, become aware that he/she isn't only anticipating your speech, but also *how* you communicate holistically—body language and all. So, you've said hello (which is essential) the next thing you say should be uttered confidently.

Even if you are saying something funny, silly, or random, say it most confidently by making eye contact and adding some excitement to the start of the conversation. When you do this, the remaining part of the small talk will follow suit. But if your starters are with anxiety and fear, it will ruin the process.

Always remember this simple yet profound rule: Start confidently, and you will finish excellently!

2. Starters Are Personal

We feel drawn toward talking about the weather first or something impersonal, but, if you are going to relate to people, you've got to have a personal touch.

When you start with something personal, you will get to learn more about the person, and they will also be interested in finding out more about you. If you don't know their names, ask, and then if you are in a particular space (maybe in an office), get to see the person's position.

Being personal is a great starter that enables you to say the next best thing because it will be a follow-up question. So, if you ask for their designation and they say, "Oh, I work in sales", you can say something about sales afterward. Then the person will have an opportunity to ask you the same thing and just like that the conversation is underway.

Be careful, however, not to confuse *personal* with *private*. Sometimes we say, "that's personal" to something when we actually mean that it's private. You'll recall from earlier chapters that it's taboo to discuss private topics during small talk. That brings us to our next point.

3. Starters Are Not Too Personal

Yes, you can be personal, but please don't be *too* personal. We gave two instances of how you can be personal, yet they're not the sort of personal questions we'd associate with private information. Don't ask a person if they are married, divorced, or single as a small talk starter. Such questions will be too personal. Great conversation starters know how to draw the line between private and personal statements or questions.

Imagine talking to someone and they ask what place on your body makes you most insecure. How would you respond? Not a great way to start a conversation, and it might ruin any good first impression the person may be trying to establish.

You've got to be careful even with jokes as starters. When you meet the person again for a follow-up conversation, you can be a bit more forward (if they are) because you've laid the foundation, but as a starter avoid being too personal.

4. Great Starters Show Genuine Interest

Another quality of great starters is the fact that the parties show real interest in each other. For example, you can show interest in the person by asking questions about things you like and suspect they may like. If you don't care about something and you add it as a starter to the conversation, you will struggle with the communication.

You will also not know how to keep the conversation interesting because you are not interested in the topic. If you don't know anything about soccer and you don't like sports, don't ask about it.

If you make this soccer idea a starter, and the other person knows quite a bit about soccer, the conversation will be one-sided. Your eagerness to make a swift change of topics might be off-putting to someone who's still excited to talk about soccer.

Stick to what you are interested in, and you will do well. If asked about something you don't know, think for a few seconds, and say you don't know. Then ask the other person to "enlighten" you. It is better to be honest than to give a false impression of knowledge. Then, when you're ready, you can steer the conversation toward a new topic without causing too much offense, as the person knows you're unfamiliar with it.

The guide above expresses the qualities of good conversation starters, which means that it will be ideal for your starters to embody such qualities. But the lesson doesn't end there; you also need to know how to start a conversation smoothly.

For that, we need to know how to transition after "hello".

Smooth Ways to Start a Conversation

Ask a General Question

You can begin by asking a straightforward question, then listening carefully for a response. Afterward, make a statement that relates to the issue and build up the conversation from there.

However, try not to be brash with too many questions because the conversation must take a natural path. Here are examples of how you can start with a simple issue:

"What brings you to New York this month?"

"What are we celebrating today?"

"Where are you from?"

"How do you know the host?"

With each of these questions, the other person can give an answer that will lead to other talks. Use the examples above as a guide.

Observe the Surroundings

Next, if your initial questions didn't provide ideas for where to go next, you can observe the area and ask about objects or surroundings to transition to new topics. Such questions are open-ended, yet they require a bit of description. If you are at a house party, you can comment on the house, make an observation about the music, or something relating to the environment.

You should be authentic and spontaneous with observational statements, yet don't be critical or start badmouthing. The essence of this starter is to get the person's opinion and build the talk from there.

"What do you think about the pink butterfly décor?"

"Do you realize how perfect the centerpiece is?"

Cold Read Something

A cold read is an educated guess about the other person based on some details you may have observed. Think about this step like making an observation yet stating an assumption. Now the fun part about this starter is that you don't have to be correct.

If you are correct, the person will be amused, and if you are not, you will be corrected, but it will add some humor to the conversation. Cold reading also shows your fun side and helps the other person feel relaxed while conversing with you.

To cold read successfully, you need to pay close attention to the person. That way you will get some essential details that will help your cold reading:

"You are not from around here, are you?"—if you spotted something different about the person's accent or dressing.

"You are quite passionate about sports, aren't you?"—if the person gave good sports predictions.

"You've been friends with the host for a long time?"—if you observe a close relationship between the person and the host of the event.

Share an Anecdote

An anecdote, or a story, will help you strike a connection with the person on an emotional level. If the person says something a bit off, you can share a humorous story, and if it engages the person, you will be off to a good start.

Here is an example of a typical conversation with a tremendous anecdotal start:

You: "Wow, what a lovely fascinator. You've got an exceptional sense of style."

Stranger: "Oh, thanks! I purchased it recently in London while out shopping with friends."

You: "You were in London? I was there a few weeks ago at this fantastic fashion store; you wouldn't believe what happened to me.

Stranger: "Haha, yes, that reminds me of what happened two days ago...

You: "Wow! That's like what happened to me...

When you start with a simple story like the example above, the other person will surely open up, and you both will have a new chat. Stories are a great connector because we all can relate to the stories other people share, so use them generously in your small talks.

Give a Compliment

Yes, we all love compliments, and these are some of the best conversation starters as well. A tribute is an excellent way of making someone else feel comfortable around you.

But you must be mindful about giving compliments because they must be real and from a particular place.

You: "Hello."

Stranger: "Hi (smiling)."

You: "You've got a lovely smile."

Stranger: "Thank you, so what brings you here?"

Bring Up Shared Interests

If you are about to talk to someone else and you observe that they've got shared interests, you can use that as a great starter.

Say you're at the coffee shop, and someone is dumping creamer endlessly into their coffee. You happen to do the same thing. You can use that as an opportunity to start a conversation.

You: "You seem to like a whole lot of cream in your coffee (little chuckle). I like it a lot too."

Stranger: "Cheers to cream in coffee (little laugh)."

Ask for Their Opinion

Another excellent option for conversation starters is to simply ask another for advice. After the initial hello, you can ask them a question that makes it easier for them to contribute to the talk from the beginning. Say you're traveling on a plane; you can ask the person seated next to you for their advice.

You: "I often feel nervous before traveling; is there something I can do to relax?"

Stranger: "Oh, that's sad; you can take deep breaths and don't focus on the flying experience."

Express Some Vulnerability

Sometimes a great way to start a conversation or small talk is through an expression of vulnerability. By vulnerability, we are not saying you should be excessively vulnerable with personal issues. We simply mean taking it upon yourself to share something with another person.

By expressing some vulnerability, you will be showing the person a side of you that he/she will want to connect with. For example, if you are at a party celebrating a product launch, and you don't know anyone. Start with this:

You: "I don't know anyone here; it is sometimes difficult for me to talk to strangers."

Stranger: "Oh, don't worry, I know most of the people here. You will find it easier to connect with someone. I'm Amy, by the way. You?"

Use a Celebrity Angle

Has someone told you that you look like a famous person? How did you feel? Flattered? If you see a person across the room, who looks like a celebrity, you can walk across to him/her and use that observation as a starter.

This approach is excellent because it is genuine in a fun and humorous way. The person will love the compliment and lighten up. If you are speaking with a woman, she will probably blush, and then a great conversation will ensue.

You: "Has anyone told you that you look like Jennifer Aniston."

64

Stranger: "Oh wow (laughs). Yeah, I think so, but I don't see the resemblance."

You: "You've both got the same hair color. Are you from around here?"

Stranger: "No, I'm from up-state. What about you?"

I cannot overemphasize the importance of smiling as an excellent tool for small talk but, more importantly, as a starter. The other person will smile back, and without saying a word, you both will have a kind of agreement, a silent acknowledgment that you've seen one another. Whether you or the other person decides to strike up a conversation is up to discretion, but at the very least, you've been connected in that fleeting moment.

Smile at the start of the conversation and then while saying the first few words. Listen, something is electrifying about a smile that sets the tone for a great discussion, especially at the beginning. In addition to everything else you have learned thus far, remember to smile from the start. Are you smiling now? Come on. Smile. Are you? There we go. Keep it up. (Works every time.).

If you start with any of the ideas above, the other person will open up to you, and then the conversation can continue. The examples above are guidelines to help you generate your own ideas. Try to experiment because every situation will not be the same. After all, it is better to be a little bit awkward than to be stiff, trying to be perfect.

Making A Good First Impression

Even though small talk starts small and seems like an easy way of communication, always remember that it is an art you must master. Small talk can open doors. Who knows where it will lead in the future? As such, you've got to make it count by making a great first impression. How do you begin?

1. Start with a small gesture (this is a building block)

Small gestures are building blocks, and they give great first impressions. Such small gestures include:

- A greeting

- A smile

- A compliment

These are little things you will always be remembered for because they lead to other in-depth parts of the conversation. A smile will lead to a "Hello," and then a "How are you," which would turn into a chat. Just start with these gestures, and you can take it from there.

2. Avoid filters

Filters are words that cause you to be excessively critical, and this kills potential in any conversation. Avoid being judgmental and trying to force your opinions down another's throat even when you know you are right.

If you tend to overthink things, please set that trait aside because this is small talk and not a philosophical conversation. Your words should be spot on, insightful, meaningful, funny, and relaxed.

Here is an example of a conversation between you and a lady who is a guest at a wedding ceremony. The talk will show how filters are used (which is wrong).

You: "Why are you wearing a white dress for the wedding?"

Woman: "Oh, white is my favorite color, and I love this dress."

You: "But this is not your wedding. Don't you think you are stealing the attention from the bride?"

Come on; if you were the lady, you would feel offended and not want to talk to the person again, right? But this wouldn't be you; I am optimistic that you will do much better!

3. You don't have to be brilliant, just kind.

People don't expect every word out of your mouth to be a revelation. To be perfectly honest, it would probably bother people. All you really need to build connections is kindness. People feel comfortable when talking to others who are nice.

Ask questions, show some interest in the other person, be friendly, exciting, and try to focus more on the other person. Don't worry about "serious" topics or complete originality. Be nice, and you will make a great first impression.

67

4. What should you say?

To make an excellent first impression, you need to think about what you will say. This thought process should happen before speaking to the person, as it will give you substance for the conversation.

You can also achieve a good first impression using this tip by creating a conversation pathway. This pathway will help you quickly move from one point to another.

But first, you need to know what you are going to say, I advise that you plan your words around concepts like:

- How the person is connected to the event

- Holidays

- Mutual acquaintances

The examples above are just a few ways you can plan your starters, and then you will build from there.

5. Build the conversation.

Making a good first impression also relates to how you create a conversation. Conversations evolve quickly as you and the other party can move from one topic to another.

When you know how to build the conversation from start to finish, you will be able to connect with the person in such a way that he/she will want to discuss it with you again in the future.

Here is an example of how you can build a conversation:

You: "So do you have anything planned for the weekend?"

Stranger: "Yes, I intend to try out the new pasta menu at the Italian restaurant down the street?"

You: "Great, I hear they've got great pasta, and it reminds me of a vacation I took to Italy last year, beautiful county!"

Stranger: "Wow, you've been to Italy. Now you are giving me vacation ideas."

You: "Oh, Italy is great. You will love the picturesque view and the food. Have you had authentic Italian food before?"

You can see that from asking about weekend plans, you both progressed into talks about food, countries, vacations, and views. This is how you build a conversation. When you create a conversation, and it naturally flows, both of you will feel at ease.

6. Exit gracefully

The way you end the talk can also affect the kind of impression you give to the other person. Most of the time, we focus exclusively on what to say and forget how to end.

The most complicated part of making small talk with someone unfamiliar is winding down the conversation. Sometimes, finding a reason to leave can be helpful, but you've got to think about it before saying it.

When you are about to end, you can use any of the examples below or use them as inspiration for stopping gracefully.

- "There's someone close standing by the entrance I need to talk to; hopefully, we will speak again soon."

- "It's been a pleasure talking to you; I have to go grab a drink now."

- "I need to make a call now, but nice chatting with you. Please excuse me."

What do people like best when they meet someone for the first time? They like it when the other person shows interest in them. Making a good first impression is a way of building relationships with others, but it all comes down to how you make them feel.

First impressions are not about words; they are mostly about connections. People will forget what you said, but they will always remember how you made them feel. All big things start with small things, like a little talk, so make the most out of it with a memorable first impression.

Conversation starters are great because they are like the bridges that connect the first "hello" to the remaining part of the conversation. The only reason you wouldn't stop at hello is that there are conversation starters, and when you are used to such starters, you won't struggle with what to say or how to say it.

In the next chapter, you will find a guide to small talk topics and what you should discuss.

CHAPTER SIX

Guide to Small Talk Topics and What to Talk About

What am I going to discuss?

Knowing the start of a conversation is not enough (I wish it were, but it isn't). If a person is great at small talk starters but doesn't know the topics to cover while speaking, he/she will have issues.

You can start a conversation confidently now (we did this in chapter 5), but we are going to learn the kind of small talk topics that are appropriate and inappropriate.

First, we will begin with safe topics and topics to avoid.

Safe Topics

The Weather

Talking about the weather may seem too predictable, but it is a fascinating topic for small talk because it is neutral and universal. Anyone can talk about the weather, and everyone has an opinion about it as well.

You can talk about the day, season, or temperature. You can also practice your small talk using weather topics. Weather topics are great in helping you get out of awkward silences as well.

Hobbies

We all have hobbies, those things we like to do, and we want to share them with others. You can introduce hobbies right after learning the person's name, and knowing what they do as this topic can add a bit of friendliness to the conversation.

Listen to the person as he/she talks about their hobbies, and if you've got questions, ask so you are clear on the idea as well.

Work

Work is a popular small talk topic that goes both ways between the sender and receiver. Getting to know what the other person does will help you understand how to make progress with the conversation.

Focus on what you want to learn about the other person's work. Work (regardless of what it is) is a crucial part of life so that it will be a fantastic topic for small talk.

Sports

Some sports topics may include favorite teams, sporting events, tournaments, bowl games, etc. Stay updated on sporting games such as soccer, football, hockey, golf, etc., if those interest you, and you'll have a consistent topic for small talk. When it's World Cup season, everyone talks about it, so keep an ear out for information.

You will find sports prominently featured in other sections of this chapter because it is a universal topic for small talk. Always focus on games you love for the smooth flow of conversation.

Family

You can also ask about family, using such conversation starters as:

"Do you have brothers?"

"How are the kids?"

Always be open about family questions and answers because engaging in this type of talk shows the depth of your communicative skills, and it helps you learn about the other person.

Hometown

You might want to ask the person about his/her hometown, and you may be requested as well. You might be from the same place as the person or know something about his/her hometown. Show interest in such topics because people will want to share such information with you.

News

The news typically concerns us all in one way or another, and by being aware of the story, you should be able to maintain basic conversations. Small talk is about building a bridge between you and the other person, so the content of the discussion will determine the strength of the bridge.

In this digital age, you don't have to rely on newspapers, as even on social media, you have access to the news to stay updated. One note, however: Be careful not to put a political spin on news topics. Keep your political opinions separate, if you can help it.

Travel

Some people like to hear and discuss vacations, so if you travel a lot, that will be an advantage for you. Ask them about the places they have visited and recommend travel destinations as well.

When you share experiences such as this, you will connect with the other person and build an excellent opportunity for a follow-up.

Arts and Entertainment

Yes, arts and entertainment topics are great for small talk! Movies, television shows, books, popular music, restaurants, etc., all make for good conversation.

This may not necessarily be the best conversation starter, but it is almost always a safe topic.

Celebrity Gossip

There are a lot of celebrities, so you don't need to know the latest with them all. However, it does help to have familiarity with the lives of some famous people.

This type of talk is appropriate for informal gatherings, casual parties, and other occasions that are not so serious. However, *do not* lead with this topic; if someone else brings it up, then go with the flow.

Topics to Avoid

Some questions are off-limits when it comes to small talk because such issues are offensive, inappropriate, or just not right. We will analyze some of these topics below in a bid to help you entirely avoid them while discussing it with someone else.

Finances

Asking the other person about how much they earn and money issues are inappropriate. It is okay to ask what a person does for a living and other positive aspects of their career, but don't ask them questions relating to their salary or bonuses.

Age/Appearance

Regardless of how a person looks, don't refer to their age or appearance. You can only do this when you know them well enough, and although age/appearance related topics may seem simple, they are also taboo topics. Don't ask the person, "How old are you?", or, "Are you pregnant?". Don't comment on the person's weight gain or loss. You can keep such observations to yourself and maintain positivity throughout the conversation.

Sex

Don't talk about sex, and don't ask questions about intimacy. Let's get real. Especially if you're talking to a stranger, you'll come off as a creep. Avoid talking openly about sexual preferences and don't make sexual references and allusions. All of these will make the other person uncomfortable and ruin the small talk.

Personal Gossip

Celebrity gossip is fair (come on, we all love a bit of Hollywood drama), but gossiping about those you know personally is off-limits. Don't gossip about others because when you do, it paints you in a bad light, and the person you are talking to may know the subject of your gossip.

Be a good person. Don't badmouth others. If you must talk about someone else within the conversation, then it should be done in good faith with positivity and kindness.

Politics

Politics poses a lot of threat to the success of small talk because you never can tell if the person you are speaking to has extreme political views. Unless you want to risk ending up in the middle of a heated and unpleasant conversation, please refrain from politics while making small talk.

Past Relationships

Past relationships could be a grey area for some people, especially if it didn't end on mutual terms. Asking people about their past relationships is being intrusive, and it can miff a lot of people.

Religion

Some topics are personal and potentially sensitive; as such, you must avoid mentioning them during a small conversation. Regardless of religious preference, you've got to understand that people have their own, and you cannot impose your ideas on them.

Always remember K.I.S.S. (Keep it short and simple).

Death

Another severe topic you must avoid is death. During small talk, please don't bring up anything related to death because the topic is typically too heavy to weigh in front of strangers.

Some topics can be very upsetting such that the person(s) you talk to might not want to have a follow-up conversation afterward. But what if you're at a funeral?

Well, you can talk about the life of the person who passed on and try to be optimistic by being available for the person who is grieving. But don't talk about death because they are trying to get over it.

Offensive Jokes

They're called offensive jokes for a reason. You'll never know who will find the jokes offensive, even if you're clearly joking and mean no harm.

Jokes that include sexist remarks, racist comments, or stereotypes should be kept under lock and key around strangers. Yes, they may be funny to you, but that doesn't mean they won't be hurtful to others.

Topic for Friends

Yes, friends are great, and you can talk to them whenever you want, but should you find yourself without a topic, here are some ideas.

Truth or Dare Questions

Truth or dare questions are also fun questions to ask friends, especially at a party or a fun event. You can enjoy entertaining banter that goes back and forth with truth or dare questions.

Some examples:

"What was your nickname in school?"

"Did you ever not make it to the bathroom in time?"

"What's the worst thing you've ever done?"

Try not to use these questions as starters also because ideally, they should come in when the talk is at its peak, and you and your friend are very comfortable with each other.

Deep Questions

Although you are talking to friends, there can also be room for some deep questions that relate to serious issues. These are the questions you ask to get an in-depth idea of how your friend is doing, especially in challenging times.

Here are a few examples:

"How are your parents?"

"What do you struggle with the most?"

"What do you think about an added degree?"

Please note that some of these questions are not great small talk starters but can be injected into the conversation while it is ongoing.

Ensure that the questions asked are at the right time and that they are appropriate for the occasion.

Would you Rather Questions

Some would-you-rather questions are humorous and witty. Such issues can also be a part of other conversations as a way of lighting up the mood. Some examples include:

"Would you prefer calls or text?"

"Would you dance uncontrollably or sing at random times of the day?"

"Would you rather get rich or marry happily?"

These questions can add a lot of fun to any conversation with your friends.

Fun Questions

Who doesn't like a fun conversation? We all do! Fun questions make us laugh, giggle, and feel relaxed while exchanging information. There are specific kinds of issues that can trigger a lot of fun.

Some examples include:

"What is the funniest memory you have from camp?"

"If you were the leader of a music group, what would be your band's name?"

Casual Questions

Causal questions are regular ones that people ask without the pressure to think about an answer, but they are also great for small talk between friends. Casual questions include everything from movies to the days of the week.

Examples are:

"What is your favorite color?"

"Have you seen any good movies lately?"

"What activities do you do in your spare time?"

"Do you watch America's Got Talent? Who's your favorite contestant or judge?"

The questions above are strategic in helping two friends engage in small talk that will lead to them also getting to know themselves better. As your friend opens up to you share your thoughts as well.

Workplace Topics

Small talk in the office or workplace seems like the easiest thing to do, right? Yet it can be challenging for some people who feel side-lined when their co-workers are discussing specific topics.

Maybe everyone is talking about football, a TV show, or an upcoming event, and you feel lost. Here is some cheerful news: You are not alone! You can change that situation at the office with the tips below and establish common ground with your colleagues.

Even if everyone is talking about something you are not familiar with or something you don't like, you can turn the tide of the small talk around to suit you. All you have to do is take charge by asking the kind of questions that suit your conversational style.

But first, you need to know some of the areas to cover, and that is what you will find below:

Please note that the tips below are questions that will help you get started on the conversation.

Pop Culture

Everyone loves pop culture! An excellent way to talk about pop culture is through movie scenes, which can help strike a conversation fast. Even if you haven't seen the Netflix series The Crown, you can nod along politely when the other person talks about or brings up a series you've watched or one you love.

Try any of these:

"I just got my Netflix subscription. What movie would you recommend I add to my list?"

"I need to binge-watch a new show. Got any recommendations?"

"I'm seeking new music to add to my Apple Playlist. What are you listening to currently?"

What do you have in Common?

Regardless of what you do within the office, you will surely have one or two things in common with someone else. You probably eat with your colleagues, commute with them, and do other things together, so there are easy ways to start small talk with this idea.

Try any of these tips:

"What is your favorite place to lunch around here?"

"I see you prefer the printer in the storage area to the one out front; I do too."

"Do you know how I can avoid walking through the construction mess on the main street?"

Office Life

Office life is something you and your colleagues have in common. This kind of topic resonates with everyone.

Try these tips:

"What's up with the smell coming from the photocopier?"

"How awesome is the new games room?"

"Please tell me I'm not the only one who has gotten stuck on the fourth elevator and almost experienced a panic attack?"

"Do you always find good parking downstairs?"

Talk About Yourself

An excellent way to engage in small talk at the office is to be yourself. Be real by talking about some of the funny yet honest issues you have that others may experience but don't want to discuss. Stop trying to be "cool". We all want you to be real so people can relate to you quickly.

These are helpful tips:

"Is anyone as obsessed with the lemon cake we get for lunch as I am?"

"I love Fridays; I tend to count down to it from Monday. I can't be the only one who does this."

Travel

Most colleagues at the office will surely want to talk about vacations (past trips and future aspirations). Vacation topics are great for small talk at the workplace.

If you have traveled a lot, don't try to rub it in with your colleagues; be modest yet excited about sharing your experiences. Show enthusiasm when they also share their experiences and try these tips:

"Where is the last place you traveled?"

"What's the next trip you have planned for summer?" "If you could take a sabbatical, where would you go, or what would you do?"

Small Talk for Business/Sales

Small talk is a vital aspect of sales, and when you add some creativity to it, you can boost your numbers. If you are in sales, or if you are an entrepreneur, you will agree that some customers are emotional buyers.

These emotional buyers understand the importance of your product to their lives but still require some connection with the seller before making a purchase. Such customers are never tired of reassurances, and when are such reassurances given? During small talk!

Small talk helps you establish a connection with clients and prospects, which in turn buys the time you need for the candidate to decide after listening to your sales pitch. The challenge with small talk for sales is knowing how to use it effectively and how to build momentum with it. You've got to know how to satisfy the prospects through a question-answer approach.

So how can you make this happen?

1. Be brief and substantive.

In the world of business, time is an essential factor, and if you want to get peoples' attention, you must show that you respect their time (even with small talk). Prospects don't care about your lengthy commentaries on how great your business model or product is, so stick to substance over long conversations.

Everything you say should be brief with specific and insightful information that will keep the attention of the prospect on you. If you do this well enough, you will have another opportunity to have an extended follow-up conversation.

2. Ask questions about the prospect's business.

By asking questions about the prospect's market space, you will be allowing him/her to lead the conversation (don't worry, you will get the right time to make your sales pitch).

When you ask about the prospect's business, it gives you an advantage because the person will feel much more comfortable with you. This step and others will provide you with an early lead for high sales.

3. Go from general to specific.

After asking about the prospect's business, you should move on from a general idea to a specific one. By "specific," I am saying you should strike a *subtle* connection between what you are offering and what the prospect will need in business.

Here is an example of a company you work for or work with that sells kitchen equipment, and you are the sales manager of the company. Your team has to sell to restaurants and families.

While making small talk with the manager of McDonald's, for example, with this step, you can draw a specific connection between the new grill set you are marketing and how it can help them at McDonald's achieve a perfect beef grill.

The general idea is "kitchen equipment," and the specific item is "grill set." I am saying that you should move from the general to the particular, as this will boost sales and help you achieve excellent small talk.

4. Ask for the prospect's views

Next, you should ask the prospect for his/her opinions on the line of business and the industry. The reason you should take this step with small talk for sales is that it will give you an insight into the possibility of closing the deal.

Discover how the prospect feels about the new product. Is the product going to solve his/her problems? When you ask this type of question, you will be getting the prospect's honest opinions, which will also contribute to your sales data.

5. Present your preposition

When your potential client is relaxed, you can shift the pathway of the conversation and move ahead into your sales presentation. Now at this point, the prospect already has an idea of what you want to say.

But you must take the initiative by presenting useful information and by showing respect for his time by being straightforward. You will find that it will be easier for you to complete the sale on a positive note using this approach.

Small Talk Questions (Bonus Section)

In this section, you will find some random short talk questions that are a valuable addition to everything else you've gained thus far. These questions incorporate varying topics.

1. What's the best career advice you've received?

2. What's your favorite restaurant?

3. Have you been to Africa before?

4. Who is your favorite person on Instagram?

5. What's your go-to comfort food?

6. If you could fly anywhere, where would you go?

7. Do you have any podcasts suggestions while we commute?

8. Are you reading a book right now?

9.   If you could watch a movie repeatedly, what would it be?

Now, these are questions that are not starters but build-ups for the conversation itself. You can always change the words to reflect the particular situation you will be in, but the point is that these questions will help you practice and what do they say about practice? It makes perfect. Knowing the current topics and those that are off-limits are probably the most crucial aspect of small talks. This realization is because a more significant part of the conversation will be on the topics you and the other person discuss.

Just as we learned what to focus on, we also unearthed what to avoid for a balanced perspective. You have done well thus far, and you must keep up with your momentum because there are still so many parts of this discourse to unravel. The next chapter is a guide on how to keep the conversation going; this should be easy because you know the topics to focus on and what to avoid, so let's get to it.

CHAPTER SEVEN

Keeping the Conversation Going

Some people will agree that starting a small talk is quite easy, especially if a person has been practicing, but how do you ensure that the conversation keeps going? How do you keep up with the other person? How can you tell what the other person will say that changes the conversation?

Well, these questions are crucial, and you will find answers to them in this chapter. Here, we will learn how not to run out of things to say (so you can maintain the flow of the conversation). You will also find the meaning of the FORD and ARE methods, respectively.

The point of all of this: avoiding awkward silences. We will begin with ideas on how not to run out of things to say.

How to Not Run Out of Ideas While Conversing

We've all had those moments during conversations when our minds go blank right in the middle of the talk. You frantically search your brain for something to say, anything, and the harder you try, the more difficult it becomes.

Awkward silence creeps in, and then you start to overthink:

"Am I incompetent at small talk?"

"What will this person think about me?"

"What's wrong with me?"

If this has happened to you in the past, you will agree that it sucks! But don't worry, now we are going to handle it (just as we have been doing thus far). You ran out of what to say because you haven't practiced well enough, and you probably got distracted while the other person was still speaking.

Practice and presence are two crucial things you must remember while building a conversation. When you are present, you will be able to utilize the ideas on how you can never run out of what to say that I am about to share with you now.

Below, you will find three major social strategies that will be very helpful.

First strategy

The first strategy is the "quick scan" approach, which serves to help you stay ahead with news and information. Every day before you head out, scan social media, online newspapers, and other exciting platforms for recent information.

The reason you are making this effort is so you can use the headlines or topics (the ones that are not sensitive or radical) as conversation starters. With this method, you have a safety net that allows you to introduce something fresh and new to the conversation.

For example, at the office you can start with:

You: "So I saw this post by Serena Williams on Instagram just before I left the house."

Stranger: "Really? What was it about?"

You: "She just launched her clothing line."

Stranger: "Wow, I've always loved Serena. Can't wait to view the collection."

With the example above, it is evident that the other person loves fashion. This method works best with people in the office or some other person that you may have an idea of what they like (sports, fashion, etc.).

Second strategy

The second strategy is the "spokes" method, which enables you to connect with anyone on varying topics. The word "spokes" for this method comes from the spokes on a bicycle tire. The spokes say that even when you don't know much about the topic of the discussion, you can roll with it. You know, like the spokes.

The small talk is the center, the spokes (topics) radiate from the center. The spokes may be different, but the conversation has to keep going, and you can introduce an issue you like if you are not familiar with the current one.

Don't stonewall the other person if they talk about hiking, for example, and you don't know anything about hiking. You don't have to continue with the hiking topic; instead, think around the issue and mention something similar to hiking that you are familiar with.

You can also play the beginner role by asking questions about hiking, as the person fills you in on the information, you will be able to flow. Overall, the spokes method teaches you that you can strike a conversation with anyone about anything.

Here is an example:

Stranger: "So have you gone hiking lately?"

You: "Wow, do people go hiking in this weather?"

Stranger: "Yes, they do."

You: "Oh nice. I prefer mountain bike races. Have you gone on one before?"

Stranger: "Yes, I have, and I enjoyed it."

The reason the spokes method works is because it is a win-win for everyone; you get to engage in great conversation without silences and awkward pauses.

However, you must always resist the urge to self-edit what you say, especially after you've said it. Let the conversation take its natural course, as it doesn't have to be perfect; it just needs to be good enough.

Third strategy

The third strategy is known as the "quick win" strategy, which teaches you not to overthink things while making small talk and that you shouldn't hesitate when responding to the other person. Hesitation will cause you to overthink, and then you will give responses such as "I can't say that" or "I don't have an answer for that." Likewise, it might lead to missed opportunities, as hesitation allows the other to dominate the discussion. As it moves forward, what you had in mind will likely become less and less relevant.

When you stop overthinking and start taking action, you will learn and grow faster. So how does this strategy work?

First, introduce yourself to any new person or people if it is a group. Then catch up on the current topic by offering your opinion.

Next, bring up interesting topics that are similar to the central discourse.

Maintain a state of curiosity about them, which will help you become interested in knowing them.

Using these steps above will enable you to achieve a quick win with your small talks. You will have more engaging conversations with a lasting impact that becomes a part of you. Such that, whenever you engage in discussion, you won't struggle with what to say.

Building social confidence is very crucial to achieving your desired goal with small talk as well. As opposed to popular opinion, everyone and anyone can build social trust, all you have to do is stick to the TWO GENERAL ideas I mentioned earlier (practice and presence).

With consistent practice and intentional presence, you will always keep up with any conversation; it will all come naturally to you with time.

The FORD Method

The letters of the FORD method represent topics that can be used in a conversation as starters with anybody.

F: Family, here you can ask about family as a way of getting to know the other person better. Now it is possible that later in the conversation, you both will make reference to family again, and if you have built a good foundation with it as a starter, it won't be awkward.

O: Occupation, remember what we mentioned in an earlier chapter? People like to talk about their work. Another way to keep the conversation going is by asking them questions about their work.

R: Recreation. Fun! We all love to talk about fun, and it is a great topic to keep the conversation going.

D: Dreams, this idea relates to speculation about the future, ambitions, and the kind of things the person will want to do. Most people feel relaxed when asked questions about their dreams, so use this as an opportunity to build great conversations.

If you want to cut off awkwardness entirely from your conversation, you must be a great listener. If the person said something, you didn't get or something you didn't understand, politely ask them to repeat it so you can grasp what they are saying. Be open to sharing just as you ask questions!

The ARE Method

The ARE method, developed by Dr. Carol Fleming, a communications expert, is excellent for small talks. This method is a three-part process with each of the letters representing the specific steps.

A: A represents "anchor", which is something that connects you with the other person. Having just met the person, the starting point of the conversation should be a comment about what you both can see and experience.

The anchor is a way of striking an instant connection with the other person by using the events or present circumstances surrounding both of you. At this "A" stage, you don't have to worry about coming up with something bright or grand. A pleasant and straightforward opening will do.

For example, if you both are at a birthday celebration for an older man, you can say, "What a beautiful night for an 80th celebration!" The "A" in the ARE method will help you start well and keep the conversation going as well.

R: R stands for "reveal", which relates to you revealing something about yourself. What you tell about yourself must correlate to how you anchored the conversation.

After the first statement about the night with the first part, you can say, "I attended some events like this last year, but the weather wasn't this beautiful."

E: E stands for "encourage", which relates to how you can encourage responses from the person by asking a question. When we do a poor job at keeping the conversation going, it is because we don't allow the other person to inject his/her opinions. Following up with our example, you can ask, "What about you? Have you attended such a celebration of life before?" When the person gives a response, the next step is to keep the ball rolling. How can you do this?

You can keep the ball rolling by asking more questions and giving follow-up comments. Always strive to strike a balance between explanations and questions as too many comments from you will restrict the other person from commenting. More so, too many questions from you will make it all seem like an interrogation.

You may ask, what if there's a lull in the conversation? Well, this is what you can do: remember the pneumonic FORM!

Yes, we've got another acronym, and it means:

Family: You can ask the person to tell you about their family. Have they had children? Grandkids?

Occupation: You can also ask them what they do for a living, what they love the most about their jobs, and some other information about their profession (not in an intrusive way).

Recreation: Recreational topics can be in the form of asking questions about vacation, what's on his/her bucket list, etc.

Motivation: With motivation, your goal is to motivate the other person to share more with you. "Do you intend on attending other such events later?"

The FORM method aims to help you avoid the typical way of carrying on with small talk, which entails annoying questions and statements such as "Hi, how are you?", "How was your week?" "I'm good". This helps you do better.

Even if you must go with this typical approach, try to fill them up with more interesting answers.

A few pointers for you:

Mention your name more than once because it is easy for the person to forget your name amid a discussion. Repetition, in this case, aids memory, and it will be a great way of making a first impression.

Always avoid one-word replies such as "Yes," "Yeah," "No". These are too abrupt, and it makes it seem like you are not willing to engage in a conversation.

Lastly, always make a clean exit by using the phrase "I need to ...", as in, "Excuse me, I need to make a quick phone call," or, "It was nice meeting you, I need to get some food now". You can also give some parting commendations such as "I enjoyed your travel stories. Hope to talk to you soon."

A very striking feature about small talk is that there is a pattern to it, and once you know the model, you can achieve success with it regardless of who you are talking to. The concepts in this chapter revealed some of these patterns and using them in addition to every other thing you've learned thus far can be very beneficial to you long-term.

We are approaching the end because the next chapter is going to be all about how you can end small talk gracefully with the other person. What can you do when you are done talking? Do you walk away? Smile and wave? How exactly should a person end small talk? Let's find out in the next chapter.

CHAPTER EIGHT

Planned Exit - Ending Small Talks Gracefully

Not many people are aware that we all need to practice how to end a discussion gracefully. As a result, people learn about the tenants of the conversation itself but fail to plan for the exit.

Yes, it is good to make an excellent first impression, but what about an excellent last impression? What should you say when the conversation winds down? How do you say it? What about the concept of a graceful exit? Is it possible to be remembered for making a fantastic lasting impression? Let's find out.

What to Say and How to Say It

There are reasons a person will want to end a conversation. They might want to end it because they have to get back to a task before or they want to run errands. It could also be that they are no longer in a chatty mood, or they want to keep things short.

Also, the way you finish off a conversation depends on the context. Maybe you ran into someone else, or perhaps you received an unexpected phone call. Generally, when you start talking with someone, it is always advisable that you have a time in mind for when you will end the conversation.

If you time yourself, you will be able to make a perfect ending. However, timing is never set in stone, especially when the conversation becomes fascinating, and you feel comfortable with the other person. Keep the conversation for as long as you can and end it well.

So, what should you say to end the small talk?

End quickly and cleanly

You don't have to say something formal to end the chat or make a grand statement. A big statement isn't called for because it will lead to you dragging on the conversation, which will ultimately make things awkward for you and the other person.

Say your goodbyes promptly cleanly and quickly, such that there is no room for an additional talk that will ruin the entire experience for you both. It is okay to say you want to go without any other window dressing. Here are some examples below:

"I have to run now. Good talking to you."

"(During a phone call) Well, that's my cue to run along now. Talk to you later?"

"Alright then (agree to what they say)."

"Enjoy the rest of the party. Goodnight".

The examples above reflect how you can end a conversation swiftly without additional comments. This step is just one way through which you can finish a discussion (we will highlight many others as we move on. The point here is that you can end quickly and cleanly.

Just leave a group discussion

The rule for a group discussion is different because you are not required to say anything in particular. If you joined a group chat at a party, then you can decide to leave after a few minutes.

All you have to do with this situation is to walk away. With group discussions, people drop in and out without obstructing the conversational flow. But if silently walking away will be too awkward for you, quietly indicate that you are leaving with a little nod or a wave.

You can also nudge the person standing next to you because they are within your reach and notify them that you are leaving.

Summarize all you've said

Another way to end the conversation in a memorable way is to summarize all you've said. This method is an excellent way to transition from the small talk to the conclusion gracefully.

Comment on the recent topic and then make a quick summary of the discussion before you indicate your exit. Here are some examples that will serve as a guide:

"Yes, clearly a lot has been happening with the company. Anyway, I should get going now. We will catch up at another time."

"You said it all; the interior designer could have done better. Let's hope it's better the next time we come to the convention. See you later."

Leave without saying too much

Don't clog the end part of a conversation with excessive discussions about irrelevant things and try not to bring up new ideas that will spark further discussions. Remember that you are at the end, and you are ready to close, so do just that without making it complicated.

Exit gracefully

Sometimes ending a small talk conversation can be tricky, which is why you should be concerned about how you complete your small talk. We will consider some tips and ideas you can implement below:

You are not the only one thinking about ending the conversation

If you are eager to end the talk, you should know that you are not alone, as the other person may also be thinking about the same thing. Most people who engage in small talk know it will end and are willing to end it at the same time you intend to.

For you to make a graceful exit, don't worry about hurting the other person's feelings when you need to end the conversation. Knowing that they may be thinking about the same thing will help you relax and get it done with ease.

Foreshadow the end

When we are about to end something, it is good to hint at it beforehand. Yes, small talk is not a very serious issue, but if you are great at it, the fact that you are about to end it might be disappointing to the other person.

For you to end gracefully, you need to cushion the impact of your departure by previewing the exit before its time. When you do this, you also program the person's mind to be prepared for the end of the chat. There are several ways to foreshadow the end of small talk; the examples below can serve as a guide.

"I promised the bride that I would introduce her to a special guest, but before I do that, let me hear your thoughts on."

Now with the example above, the speaker has foreshadowed the end of the chat already by informing the person that he/she will be heading the bride's way soon (we are assuming this is at a wedding). Some other examples:

"I can't wait to go try the pastries over there, but what do you think about the décor?"

"I will be visiting the display stand right after you tell me all about the new product your firm launching next week."

Make an introduction

Another way to end small talk gracefully is by making a very organic introduction. This step enables you to make a smooth exit by introducing the other person to someone else, then ending the conversation.

Here, you give the person you were chatting with an opportunity to connect with someone else as you make your graceful exit.

But you must be mindful because you are not expected to introduce just about anybody, you must add someone who is within the discourse and someone who can be a mutual contact to you both.

If the other person is talking excitedly about the decoration or interior design at the event, for example, you could introduce him/her to the interior designer. Now the right way to execute this is by being conscious of timing, presence, and the person you will introduce.

Please don't walk away from the person entirely to bring the person you want to introduce. This step means that if you are going to use this pattern, you will have to start scanning the room for possible introductions while still chatting with the person.

Some examples you can utilize includes:

"Hey, there's the chef. Want to meet him?"

"You need to connect with this DJ, so he can show up for your next party."

Give a rationale for ending the talk

With motives, you will be explaining why you are going off and indicate that you have enjoyed the chat. Here, you can signal the end of the talk and increase the odds of a follow-up conversation in the future.

Examples:

"I love this conversation, but I just noticed it's 8:30, and I have to be home by 9. Can we continue with this some other time?"

"Oh my, the weather just changed, and, if I don't leave now, I will get drenched by the rain."

From the examples above, we can agree that the rationales provided by the speakers express their disappointment at ending the chat, signals their exit, and also shows how regrettable it is for them to leave. Using this method is graceful and will help you achieve a great connection with the other person.

Use immediate surroundings

You can also use your immediate surroundings to construct your ending organically. For example, if there is a drink stand by where you are standing, you can encourage the other person to grab a drink, knowing that you both will get mixed up in the crowd or encounter others for a chat.

If it is a pool party, for example, you may suggest that you both head out to the pool area, and, by doing this, you can move on gracefully from the small talk. But before using this style, make sure you have said all you need to say, and you are ready to end the conversation as well.

Making an Excellent Last Impression

People remember the beginning of a thing and the end as well, but typically have trouble remembering the middle. Think about when you read a novel, and it started with a lot of suspense; you will remember all of it after reading—but as time goes on, you'll likely only remember the beginning and end, and, perhaps the climax.

The novelist created balance with the beginning and end, and you must do the same. Don't spend so much time thinking about how to make a first impression while ignoring efforts to make a good last impression. You will find tips that will help you make a good final impression.

1. Make physical contact twice before leaving.

In most or all cases, making physical contact with the person just before leaving aids bonding between the two parties. A handshake is a sign of great rapport and makes you memorable; it also contributes to making you very likable.

Give a warm yet confident handshake just as you are about to part ways, and, if the person is someone you are familiar with, you can give a subtle hug. In some cultures of the world, pecks on the cheeks are ideal when meeting strangers (so be conscious of cultural implications as well).

Your handshakes should be firm (this will make it a very memorable handshake). Ensure to connect your fingers, and they should be flat rather than cupped so you can touch their palms. There is so much power in a firm handshake.

2. End with eye contact and a smile.

We have talked about the importance of making eye contact and smiling in previous chapters, and these non-verbal signs are vital while ending the discussion.

Always look at the person in the eye directly and give them the impression that you are open, warm, and straightforward. As you make eye contact, smile warmly, and let that be the image the person holds in his/her mind about you.

Making eye contact also enables you to internalize the person's facial features such that when you see him/her somewhere else again, you would remember the small talk and take it up from there. A smile is a tremendous non-verbal communicative tool for a memorable last impression.

3. Move with intent.

Avoid standing there, shifting your weight because you are hesitant to leave. You've got to move with some intention by being friendly yet firm with your goodbye. Know what you will do next, so you could mention it subtly as you prepare to leave.

By moving with intent, I mean that, if you need to move across the room to talk to someone else, you should know it. When you are unintentional about leaving, it will lead to a lot of awkwardness, which will also ruin any attempt on your end for an excellent last impression.

Some examples include:

"It's been a pleasure talking to you; now I need to get to my car. Thank you."

"Wow, what an experience you had! I hope we get to talk about this again. I need to catch up with the groom over there. Thank you."

4. Don't cut the other person short.

Sometimes, when we are ready to end a conversation, our minds get so one-tracked that we inappropriately cut the other person off even while he/she is still talking. Yes, we know you are in a hurry, and you want to leave, but you also want to leave a tremendous last impression, which requires you to show respect for the other person.

For you to avoid cutting people short, you must take control of the conversation by giving signals that you are ready to leave. If the person still talks afterward, allow him/her finish, and then end the talk (but don't cut the person off).

Cutting the person off will send a wrong signal to him/her about your personality, and it is generally a rude approach. I know some people might go on and on talking, but then you've got to be tolerant.

However, if you MUST cut them off (this is in rare cases when you need to leave, and the person wouldn't stop talking) then you can use the ideas below:

"I hate to interrupt your stream of thought, but I have to leave."

"Sorry for butting in, but if I don't talk to the principal now, he will leave the premises."

"What an inspiring story, it's so sad I can't stay to hear it all."

5. Thank the person.

As you get ready to end the conversation, remember to thank the person by looking them in the eye and saying, "Thank you." More specifically, you've got to thank them for their time, or a great chat.

Now you can say thank you twice: when you realize that you are about to end the conversation and when you intend to leave the scene. As you say thanks, make the other person feel like you have had a great time.

Some examples are:

"Thank you for your time this evening; it was lovely chatting with you."

"Thank you for your wonderful food suggestions; I will have a great time with the recipes."

6. Keep open-ended conversations.

Another way to make an excellent lasting impression at the end is to keep an open discussion, so the next time you meet this person, you both will have significant common ground to pick up from where you left off. The other person will be excited about continuing the conversation and even ponder on how the next discussion will be. Now, keeping the conversation open-ended may not apply to all situations, but if it does apply to yours, make it count.

We have achieved a balanced narrative thus far with how to start and how to end the small talk with anyone gracefully. Listen, if you stick to all these ideas and concepts, you can hold a conversation anywhere. We're getting close to the end, but there's still more to discuss. In the next chapter, we focus on how you can make genuine connections with people.

CHAPTER NINE

Making Genuine Connections with People

The experiences we have with people are based on the connections we build with them. When we make great connections with people, everything else relating to how we converse with them becomes more comfortable. You can initiate small talk now, and you can end it, but the question is, can you make a *genuine* connection with people—the kind that builds lasting friendships?

Do you know the kind of questions that will lead to deeper connections? What are the signs that you are connecting with someone? Can small talk become even more meaningful?

If you observe the pattern with this book, I tend to ask you a lot of questions because that is one of the quickest ways to learn a lot about life. Questions teach you two things:

1. What you know

2. What you don't know

When you answer a question correctly, it means you understand the concept, and when you don't, you know what you should get to know.

With the questions I have asked, you will be able to decipher if you know these concepts and if you don't.

We will begin with small talk perspectives/approaches that will help you strike a connection with people.

Small Talk Perspective/Approaches

Small talk is one of the swiftest and most organic ways through which you can strike a connection with people. As you know, there are varying ways through which you can use small talk that can be advantageous to you, but we are not going to go through a repetitive circle again.

What this section aims for is to show you some approaches to establishing genuine connections between people. Using these ideas and all other concepts you've learned thus far can help you become a much better communicator while connecting with others. Shall we begin?

Use what they say

An excellent approach for small talk is to use what the person says as an anchor for the conversation. This approach puts the spotlight on the discussion on the other person and helps you retain a perfect relationship with him/her.

Always look to intentionally use what they say as a catalyst for the conversation going forward and help them maintain a lead on the conversation by using their words and suggested topics.

Find out what makes them special

We all have qualities that make us special, distinctions that set us apart from others. When someone identifies this exceptional quality in us, we feel welcomed, loved, and appreciated.

You can genuinely strike a connection with someone else just by identifying what makes them unique and commending them for it. It doesn't have to be something based on character (you just met the person); it can be personality-based or a visible attribute they portray.

Don't push people to see and embrace your perspective

Another perspective you must consider is to avoid imposing your view on other people. Yes, you have strong opinions, and you want the whole world to hear you. Nonetheless, small talk is not a place to indoctrinate people. It's a place to build connections, one to learn—not teach.

Always give room for the other person's opinions and seek common ground with him/her. We will discuss more on common ground in another section in this chapter.

Reveal something personal

Yes, this is an approach of small talk that will help you make genuine connections with people. When you share something personal, you are sending a message to the person that you are open to a relationship, which is the essence of great small talk.

But please be mindful of what you share (if you go with this approach). Don't share overly personal things (for example, a miscarriage or the death of a child). Avoid sharing painful memories as soon as you meet a person. Get to know them first. You could share challenges at work or your struggle to buy a good piece of property. You mustn't scare the other person away by revealing too much too soon.

Questions leading to deeper connections

Not all inquiries lead to deeper connections, some are "yes" or "no" questions, and some others require only succinct direct answers. But if you are keen on getting connected with someone else, you must intentionally ask questions that will lead to deeper connections.

Below, you will find some of these questions which go beyond the surface and help you reach the person at a well-connected level.

1. "Why do you live in this neighborhood?"

2. "What is your vision for this non-profit?"

3. "How do you feel about your life situation?"

4. "Which new skill would you love to learn?"

5. "Who do you admire in history?"

6. "What would you be known for if you were a celebrity?"

Ways to Make Small Talk More Meaningful

Whereas some discussions are meaningful, others are simply exchanging pleasantries. You should strive to make discussions meaningful, and cast aside the stigma that small talk inherently has: that it's simply a waste of time. It's not—not if you're striking up a substantive conversation. This isn't always best, however. For example, you might have no intention of striking up a conversation with a stranger in the future (for reasons best known to you), in which case, you will want to stick to an ordinary and drab conversational style.

But if you seek a relationship with the person and you want to continue with the conversation, you will have to do more. By more, we mean take a cue from the examples below because they can be helpful.

Celebrate successes

If you want to make small talk with others more meaningful, you must celebrate their progress as they share them with you. By success, I am referring to the little bits of information they share with you that are an indication of their progress.

You can inject some exclamations that show your excitement for them; some examples include: "Wow," "Amazing," or, "That's so good." If a person tells you that he traveled to the Vatican City for vacation and met the Pope, don't let it slide. Respond to the information by celebrating his/her success through such exclamations.

Focus on engagement

You can also get a more meaningful conversation by focusing on engagements between the two of you. What are the points of the discussion that you both seem to enjoy the most? Focus on those points and dig further into them.

You will find that your small talk is even more meaningful because you are not conscious of what gets less attention from both of you.

The gift of going first

For you to have a more in-depth conversation, you need to give the gift of going first by choosing to share something personal or vulnerable. When you do this, the other person will take your cue and do the same. Sometimes, between both parties, one person is waiting to see if the next person will take the first step.

By sharing something deeply, you will be having a more meaningful conversation with a deep-rooted connection such that the follow-up talk will flow naturally. People often respond in kind to such gestures, so take the step for a more rewarding and bonding experience.

Don't (always) fill a silence gap

You mustn't superimpose your words by filling the silence gap all the time. If you do this, the other person will become lazy and would leave you to take the lead, ultimately making the conversation one-sided.

Give room for the person to take the lead as well and be content with following sometimes. Even if you know what to say every time silence creeps in, resist the urge, and allow the talk to flow naturally.

Encourage elaborate descriptions (if you've got time)

If you've got time for small talk, you can allow the other person to give detailed explanations, which will also aid a fascinating conversation. Encourage the person when he/she is showing enthusiasm about a topic by using sentences like "Go on," "This must be interesting," and "Wow, I didn't know that."

Remember that the caveat with this step is that it should be used when you are sure you've got time for it. It wouldn't make sense for you to lead the person on and cut him/her off halfway by saying you want to leave.

Signs You Are Connecting with Someone

How can you tell that the above ideas work? How will you know when you have connected with someone in the course of the conversation?

In this final section, you will discover the signs that show how well you are connecting with someone else.

Please note that for some of the ideas below, there are exceptions, and I will indicate these exceptions (if any).

1. Notice a slight smile

A great way to tell that you are connecting with someone is if he/she gives you a little smile while you speak. That smile is a sign that they genuinely enjoy your company, and they love conversing with you. Make sure to return the favor by smiling while they speak, as well.

2. Do you both have some common ground?

Even if you both have little disagreements, at some point during the small talk, you should have moments of common ground as this is a sign of great connection. Most of the time, social setting contributes immensely in providing common ground because you both can draw on the surroundings for talking points.

For example, do you both like the party setting? Are you both colleagues at the office? If the people around the venue are there for the same reason as you, then there is a higher chance of you both having common ground.

If you struggle to achieve common ground with the other person, then it might mean that there is no connection between the two of you. But all hope isn't lost, you can lean in with them by taking what they say and endorsing it to aid common ground (this step can be utilized if you are keen on striking a connection).

3. Is the person making eye contact?

Eye contact is significant when making small talk because it is a visible sign of connection. Of course, by now, you know the difference between eye contact and staring, so while we don't want the person staring at us, we certainly don't want them looking away either.

If the person intentionally avoids making eye contact, then he/she hasn't connected with you. You can help the person at some point to mirror you by also making eye contact with them, but if they don't reciprocate, it means they don't want to talk further.

4. Are they digging deeper into the conversation?

When you start talking, try to find out if the person is making attempts at getting to know more about you or what you are talking about. After the initial "hello," you should track the individual's responses to questions you ask and how they answer yours.

If you do all the talking and they don't ask further questions, then it means they are not interested in the conversation. However, you can be sure of making a connection if, after the first three minutes, they are responding well to you.

5. Are they willingly sharing information with you?

When a person willingly shares information with you without you asking, it is a sign that they are connected to you. It's a sign of comfort level as well.

On the flip side, some people withhold information even when you ask, and it could be a sign that they are not comfortable with you—or simply that they are not as well-versed in small talk. If you sense this withdrawal, you can reach out to them by also sharing information and watch to see how they react.

6. Do they mirror you?

Mirroring is crucial, and while speaking, you should pay attention to the other person's body movements. Do you remember when we talked about mirroring in a previous chapter? According to studies on communication, humans tend to reflect each other when they are interested or when they have made a connection with someone else.

Sometimes we become so comfortable with the person that mirroring becomes a subconscious act. Mirroring helps us reassure the other person that we love being around them. But if you are making hand gestures and the other person stays stiff, it could be a sign that they want to end the conversation.

7. Are they following the details you share?

Another sign to look out for is if they follow the details you share. When conversing with a person, if he/she often forgets what you say, then it is a sign that you haven't connected with him/her.

But if the person is enthusiastic about your narratives, stories, and opinions, then you've got yourself a great small talk buddy. To check this sign, you can say something repeatedly and then ask them. If they don't understand, then they haven't been listening, and that also means you haven't struck a connection with them.

8. Do they make body contact?

Yes, when people have struck a connection with you, they start to feel comfortable enough to make body contact. Some people, regardless of what you do, will never make body contact because they seek minimal interaction with you.

So, such people will not give you a handshake, hug, or even touch you slightly. If you extend your hand, they may take it less firmly than expected. But, on the bright side, if the person has made a connection with you, they will not shy away from professional body contact.

Please note that in some cases, a person might be pleased with you but has issues with making body contact with strangers. So please don't take it personally when a person doesn't reciprocate your body contact gestures.

9. What about the "feet rule"?

There is an old rule that states that when a person is interested in you, he/she will point their feet towards you while speaking. Yes, it is an old saying, but it still holds a lot of truth. While conversing, take a split second to look down if the person's feet are pointed in your direction. If it is so, then it is a good sign; it means the person is mirroring you successfully and is ready to move in whatever direction you take the conversation.

On the contrary, if their feet are pointing in another direction, it means that they are no longer interested and want to end the conversation. Please note that this is an old rule, and it is not set in stone (people can adjust their body parts as they deem fit), which means it may not apply to every situation.

10. Do they drop their guard around you?

A good sign that you have made a connection with some is when they drop their guard around you. With some people, you can feel the walls around them still intact, such as folding their arms across their chests, stiffening their shoulders, or crossing their legs.

But once you spot a fully relaxed person around you, then you know that they have dropped their guard and they are free with you. This sign ultimately translates into a great connection with the person.

Connecting with people is an enriching experience. It's how we ultimately make all of our lifelong friends. So now you know how to build such authentic connections, which will also enable you to succeed at making small talk with anyone anywhere.

The next chapter is the last one in this book. You've got the foundation. You've got all the skills you need. Now we simply need to perfect those skills. We're talking about mastery.

CHAPTER TEN

Mastering the Art of Small Talk

We have learned the most basic and in-depth ideas on the art of small talk, which has contributed immensely to helping you know how to begin the conversation and how to make the most out of it long-term. I've always encouraged you to put your skills to the test, making small talk in the field. Still, even if you feel like a pro, there's always more work to be done to become a master at something.

We'll begin with a reminder of why we make small talk. What makes it worth your time? And of course, we'll discuss what you can do to master it. Some of the ideas you will discover below may sound familiar, but we will be considering these concepts from the standpoint of gaining mastery.

The Art of Small Talk and Why It's Worth Your Time

For you to gain mastery of anything, you must know its worth! Of what importance is this discourse to you? When you fully understand the reason small talk is crucial, you will start to make conscious efforts towards ensuring that you gain mastery.

Think about all the non-familiar relationships that became familiar ones. What was the tipping point for such connections? How did such people move from being strangers to best friends? The answer is quite simple: small talk!

Now, in addition to being able to help you retain perfect friendships, the benefits of the small talk below will also empower you to take the concept of mastery seriously. Let's discover more, shall we?

1. Small talk is spontaneous.

One of the benefits of small talk to you and the reason it is worth learning is the fact that it is unplanned. With speeches and other communication patterns, you will be required to carry out some preparatory exercises because you are expected to meet a certain standard.

However, with small talk, you must be as good as the last one you had and build on it consistently. The spontaneity of small talk also removes whatever kind of pressure you may feel to be anything other than yourself.

2. Small talk can inspire new ideas in you.

Yes, with small talk, you are consistently inspired with new ideas because you will be interacting with new people who have varying opinions about life and work.

If you pay close attention to the content of the conversations, you will agree that there is always something new to learn. Your perspective on specific topics will also often change because the interaction is the foundation of education.

3. It helps you embrace your real value.

When you are engaged in small talk, you will get to see yourself through the lenses of another person. As the person commends you and points out the value in what you say, you will start to embrace your real value.

Most people trivialize their opinions and their view of the world because they erroneously think they are insignificant. However, when you chat with someone for a few minutes and he/she says "Wow, you've got an amazing perspective", you will learn to value that comment, which affects how you see yourself.

4. You become a better admirer.

Small talk also empowers you to become a better admirer of others. Some people are not great at connecting with others because they don't engage in what they perhaps believe to be a fruitless conversation, and they are isolated.

When you start sharing your thoughts with others, when you begin to connect with people, you will fall in love with the diversity and uniqueness of human nature. This idea also influences your ability to be a better admirer of people who acknowledge their flaws but respect their opinions.

5. It helps you create lasting impressions.

We dedicated an entire chapter to learn how to create lasting impressions because it is essential. Those lasting impressions become the springboard from which follow-up conversations are birthed and relationships formed.

6. You also become a people's person.

One of the hallmarks of leadership is a person's ability to be a people's person. As a people person, you can relate on any level, and this will help you lead with purpose.

Imagine being a manager who has occasional small talk with subordinates at the office. You will agree that through those little conversations, you will get to know more about the people who work for you and know how to harness their abilities for the good of the firm, and better yet, for their good.

7. You wouldn't struggle with holding a viable conversation.

The struggle to maintain an excellent discussion with new people is real, especially in this digital age. But a person who is proficient in the small talk will not struggle with conversational patterns. Such people will not only be great with small talk starters, but they will also know how to take other people along.

Small talk helps you build a conversation from start to finish without awkward silences and other mannerisms that affect the flow of a proper conversation.

8. A great career booster.

Within the corporate world and other workplaces, those who are great at small talk are those who get to move up the ladder quickly because they are good at connecting with people.

Such people will get the attention of top management because every company will consider both your hard and soft skills. What you do for the company/business is your hard skill, and your ability to communicate effectively with your colleagues and those you lead constitute your soft skills. A combination of both skillsets will serve as a significant career boost!

Best Practices to Improve Your Conversational Skills

If you ever struggled with conversational skills, you would need to start indulging more in small talks. As you apply this principle, you will notice a significant improvement in your communication skills and your ability to reach out to strangers.

Small talk completely transforms the way you view communication. You will move from seeing it as a stressful process to embracing it as a bridge that connects you with others. It is, for this reason, you must become intentional about mastering the art of small talk.

We have laid the foundation for mastery with the worth of small talk and its value to your experience. Now we will move on to learning all about good practices that will improve your conversational skills.

The practices you will discover below are not ideas you should implement once and forget. These are ideas that should be repeatedly utilized until they become a part of you. You can come back to this chapter every time you feel the need to upgrade your small talk skills.

Think of the ideas below as habits that can only become a part of you when you do them consciously. No one was born with an excellent ability to execute small talk; we all must deliberately learn and trust that the more we put in the effort, the better we become.

1. Face your fears.

Introverts are not the only ones who struggle with making small talk, as it can be intimidating for anyone. However, due to how important it is, we must all learn how to make it work, and the first step to doing that is by facing your fears.

You've got to highlight the major reason why you don't like small talk and then plan to conquer that fear. It could be that you don't feel comfortable around strangers, so what can you do if that's the case? Spend more time with the people you don't know!

When you face your fears, they can no longer limit you!

2. Use a friend.

To master the art of small talk, you've got to practice a lot, and you should work closely with a friend so you can feel comfortable. When you visit your friend, engage in small talk over a wide range of topics that may cut across the weather, food, vacation, etc.

Use this step whenever you have the opportunity, and you will find that you are gaining mastery over time. Talking with a friend will help you handle the sweaty palms and knotted feeling in your stomach caused by anxiety over making small talk.

3. Ask questions.

When you make it a habit to always ask questions, you will do the same whenever you are making small talk. If you get to a new place where things are very different, learn how to ask questions, as this will help you build confidence.

Regardless of where you are (with a larger or smaller group) or a one-on-one conversation, if you ask the right questions, you will build your skills. Questions help you move the conversation from the surface level to a real place where a relationship can thrive.

4. Set your mind right.

Your mind plays a crucial role in the success or failure of small talk. If you always hold the opinion that you cannot make small talk successfully (maybe because of past mistakes), no matter how well you practice, you will struggle.

So set your mind right by telling yourself that you can do it! Don't allow the failures of the past to get in the way of your commitment. Before going for an event, make up your mind that you will make small talk and tell yourself that regardless of who you speak to, it will be successful.

5. Make a game of it.

Sometimes for you to master a concept, you've got to play with it so you can enjoy the process. Trick yourself into seeing small talk as fun, and commit at least an hour to meet someone new and learning something about them.

Your mind will experience a shift, and the more you engage in this kind of game, the more natural small talk becomes. Give yourself points every time you get it right with someone and build on your previous success to get better.

6. Be yourself!

Don't try to be someone else who is excellent at small talk in the office because you think he/she is better than you. You didn't read this entire book so you could imitate someone else now, did you?

You read this book to empower yourself, and you have gained that empowerment. What's next? You've got to be authentic. Don't fake an accent because you want to "appear" relatable to the other person. All you have to do is to be you. Be original and be excellent!

7. Lower your expectations.

You have read this book that has prepared you for the future with small talk, but other people don't have access to such publications; as such, they still deal with specific conversational challenges.

It will be wrong for you to show up to discuss with such people and expect them to be as good as you. Please minimize your expectations of others and go with the flow of the talk.

Don't add to their awkwardness by laughing at their mistakes and putting a stop to the conversation because you don't find them "interesting." Keep expectations at a minimum, and you will be able to gain mastery of small talk.

8. Don't be on the sidelines.

Being on the sidelines means sticking to someone else and standing behind them (hiding) while they make small talks. You are too good to be standing on the sidelines, and you have been groomed to do better.

Don't be a sidekick. Don't be a wallflower. Don't stand in another person's shadow because if you do, you will never gain mastery. You may have accompanied your friend to an event, but after a few minutes of arriving together, find your way around the venue and make contact with new people.

9. Take responsibility for the process.

You must take responsibility for the conversational process whenever you are talking to someone else, so you learn how to take charge of small talk. Don't blame the other person when the conversation becomes dull; don't attribute it to something the person said or did.

If you must gain mastery of small talk, you must be willing to take responsibility. Taking responsibility will propel you to give your best and utilize all the ideas shared thus far in this book.

10. Don't stop practicing.

Above all, don't stop trying! I am still harnessing the power of small talk even today because I am always practicing for varying scenarios.

When you practice well enough, you will become confident, and this will empower you to set the tone for your conversations.

Consistent practice is the key to mastering the art of small talk, and with the ideas shared in this chapter, you can rest easy knowing that you are on the path to being an expert in it.

Oh, what a moment it is right now! We have finally come to the end of a fantastic journey, and it feels rewarding. You have been such a good sport, and I believe you deserve a pat on the back. We will round off this journey with a concluding section that will propel you to action.

FINAL WORDS

Now you know what to say next after hello!

The key message for this book is how you can engage in small talk while building better relationships. We started like we were on a journey by analyzing some of the key reasons why people struggle with making conversation with strangers. Fear, anxiety, and shy personas were some challenges we discussed, and then we moved on to solutions.

This book has taught you the definition of small talk as a foundational part of the discourse and how you can overcome shyness as an individual. You unearthed the value of the social skill code while gaining insight into the concept of non-verbal communication.

Knowing what comes after hello is crucial for the success of small talk. You wouldn't feel stuck while communicating because you know how to maintain conversations.

Planning a graceful exit is also vital because as much as you want it to end, you also want to be remembered fondly. Overall, you have gained in-depth insight into how to master the art of small talk, and this is the biggest lesson to glean from this material.

From the start, I promised you that you would enjoy the process and become enthusiastic about small talk. I hope that's true now, but what you gain from this text is ultimately up to you. It's out of my hands.

The solution mentioned at the start was encapsulated in one word, "Enjoy." Now, if you enjoyed reading, you will surely enjoy making small talks, which ultimately will help you get better every day. I'll say it again: Perfection is the enemy of the good. Don't expect it immediately after reading this book. Seek it. Strive for it. Then learn to let it go and accept good enough.

You'll see progress if you practice. Remember that this isn't magic. This is a process. You must engage with it as it engages with you. Over time, you'll improve.

Pressure will pave the way for disappointments. That is not in the spirit of this book. I want you to feel comfortable and relaxed knowing that it will take consistent practice for you to become a master.

Nonetheless, if there's one thing that's most important about this book, what do you think that would be?

It's this: You can hold a conversation (small talk) with anyone, anywhere. I want this idea to be palpable to you; it should be within your mind all the time, so you are prepared. Remember this message when you are at a party wondering if you can strike up a conversation with someone standing next to you.

You can start small talks with people you've just met, and you can do it without fear of the unknown. You are ready to build new friendships with people that will add color to your world.

Small talk is an integral part of everyday life. It's easy to dismiss it as something pointless, something that will get you nowhere. In truth, though, it contributes to your well-being and happiness. You will probably miss out on meeting your soulmate if you have a fear of small talk. Yes, your soulmate!

Also, remember that the principles discussed in this book do not only apply to face-to-face interactions. This is the digital age, and, as such, much of your communication will happen online. You can socialize just about anywhere these days: Facebook, Instagram, YouTube, email, Snapchat, Kik, WhatsApp, text messages, etc. Through such social platforms, you can build confidence and master the art of conversing with others.

As we round off this journey, I want to reinforce the power of confidence. You need to build confidence to fight off the impact of negative thoughts. They are not the reality you make them out to be. To put it in perspective, when you think positively, you become excited about meeting someone and learning from them.

That positivity transforms into self-confidence because you are in a great mental space for interaction. Don't worry about being boring; you are a worthy person who has got a unique point of view and a particular way to say it. More so, the people you speak to could also be as shy as you are, so why not make the best out of the situation?

Whenever you feel nervous or anxious before meeting people, get excited about the encounter, and visualize a successful talk. Happiness will turn your trepidation into something positive while leading the way by interacting, engaging, and learning something new.

The fact that this book ends here doesn't mean I can't give you additional tips for success. I want you to go into the world, feeling empowered and ready to speak passionately.

Here's another great idea for you; try practicing stoicism as a way of seeing things from a more rational viewpoint. We all wear pants the same way, one leg in at a time, so don't try to rush things. Focus on the present moment when you are conversing and avoid getting caught up on past awkwardness and what-ifs that birth irrational fears.

You will achieve more with your practice when done in a familiar environment. Don't start by attending social events you are not interested in and stick to settings where you can thrive easily. The aim is for you is to have fun and enjoy the process, so ask yourself, what are my interests? What do I believe? These questions will make it easier for you to cultivate relationships with like-minded people.

Recall our discourse on the four-ears or four-sides model that provides you with the idea that a statement made by another person can mean different things. The message is:

1. Factual Information: Desire to accurately state information.

2. Appeal: To appeal to you or seek command or receive advice from you

3. Relationship: To refer to an aspect of your existing relationship.

4. Self-Revelation: Divulge something about themselves (motives, values, emotions, likes/dislikes, etc.)

Don't forget to interpret non-verbal clues and body language of the people you interact with at events. Keep an eye on their gestures, facial expressions, tone of voice, and posture. You should also soften your body language while in conversation, so your communication isn't misinterpreted as aggressive.

You must seek to provide a positive experience both for yourself and the other party. Smile more, sit up straight and show excitement (this is so important), would you enjoy small talk with someone who looks bored? Of course not!

In addition to excitement, be interested in what the people are saying by listening emphatically. Be an active participator, be positive, friendly, and be a warm person. Be the person that everyone loves to connect with.

Another way you can win with small talks is to keep the conversation going by asking open-ended questions. Questions about the weather are not open; they are direct questions that will not lead to exciting discussions. Also, avoid controversial topics that will lead to overly passionate outbursts (examples of such issues are politics and other adverse problems).

Please don't get confused. Here is a piece of advice that can help you strike a balance; tie in the conversation starter to the occasion, event, or location. Talk about the décor, the colors, the main reason for the game, the organization, etc. This way you will be on the safe yet exciting side.

Get to talk about hobbies, art, what brought your acquaintance to the event, and how they know the host. These are topics that will inspire a fascinating conversation between you and the acquaintance. Prepare conversation starters ahead of time as well to avoid stress. By preparing, you will be ready for anything. Don't focus solely on the content of the conversation and forget how to end it properly. When you end correctly, you open an opportunity for future discussions. If you meet the person again, you both can continue from where you left off.

You can be proactive with message continuance by sending a follow-up message soon after to maintain the connection. With proper follow-up, you can build new and lasting relationships as an adult in the digital age.

We have shared so much thus far, and I hope you are pumped up and ready to go! Above all, take great pride in executing the knowledge gained because think about it, what is the usefulness of information if it isn't applied?

This should be your formula going forward: READ = INTERNALIZE = EXECUTE = REPEAT!

Best wishes.

RESOURCES

English Club, (2019), Small Talk Practice 2: At the office Retrieved November 4, 2019 from https://www.englishclub.com/speaking/small-talk_practice2office.htm Bridges, F. (2019, April 25).

What to Say After "Hello" Retrieved November 4 2019, from https://www.nicknotas.com/blog/what-to-say-after-hello/ Frost, A. (2019, July 24).

The Ultimate Guide to Small Talk: Conversation Starters, Powerful Questions, & More. Retrieved November 4, 2019, from https://blog.hubspot.com/sales/small-talk-guide Callahan, J (2018, May 31)

10 Nonverbal Cues That Convey Confidence at Work. Retrieved from https://www.forbes.com/sites/jacquelynsmith/2013/03/11/10-nonverbal-cues-that-convey-confidence-at-work/#1f5b763f5e13 Smith, J. (2013, March 11)

Stop overthinking and Never Run Out of Things To say Retrieved November 4, 2019 from https://goodmenproject.com/featured-content/stop-overthinking-never-run-out-things-say-lbkr/ Schiffer, V. (2019, June 13).

The Art of Misunderstanding & The 4 Sides Model of Communication. Retrieved November 4, 2019, from https://www.medium.com/seek-blog/the-art-of-misunderstanding-and-the-4-sides-model-of-communication-7188408457ba Amintro, (2019, July 30).

The Art of small talk: how to start and keep a conversation going, Retrieved November 4, 2019 from https://www.amintro.com/life/art-small-talk-start-keep-conversation-going/ Hertzberg, K. (2017, June 20).

Small Talk 101 for Shy People in the Office. Retrieved November 4, 2019, from https://www.grammarly.com/blog/small-talk-tips-for-introverts/ Eduard, (2012, April 30).

The Best Conversation Starters Retrieved November 4, 2019 from http://conversation-starters.com/ Khuu, C. (2018, October 8).

15 Tips to Get Better at Small Talk. Retrieved November 4, 2019 from https://www.success.com/15-tips-to-get-better-at-small-talk/

The Art of Small Talk. Body language. Retrieved November 4, 2019, from https://www.the-art-of-small-talk.com/bodylanguage.html Sedghi, A. (2019, February 11).

37 Conversation Starters that make You Instantly Interesting, Retrieved November 4, 2019 from https://www.readersdigest.ca/health/relationships/interesting-conversation-starters/ Johnson, P. (2016, August 11).

7 Ways to Make a Big Impression with Small Talk, Retrieved November 4, 2019 from https://www.heysigmund.com/7-ways-to-make-a-big-impression-with-small-talk Hey, S. (2019).

Small Talk Practice 2: At the Office, Retrieved November 4, 2019 from https://www.englishclub.com/speaking/small-talk_practice2office.htm

How To Be Better At Small Talk, Retrieved November 4, 2019 from https://www.forbes.com/sites/francesbridges/2019/04/25/how-to-be-better-at-small-talk/#318291135ca5 Holiday, R., & Hanselman, S. (2016).

Small Talk for Big Sales, Retrieved November 4, 2019 from https://www.sellingpower.com/2010/02/02/8361/small-talk-for-big-sales Craig, B. (2010)

Keep Conversations Flowing With the FORD Method, Retrieved November 4, 2019 from https://curiosity.com/topics/keep-conversations-flowing-with-the-ford-method-curiosity/ Ashley, H. (2018, February 8).

Stop Overthinking and Never Run Out of Things To Say, Retrieved November 4, 2019 from https://goodmenproject.com/featured-content/stop-overthinking-never-run-out-things-say-lbkr/ Jeff, C. (2018, May 31).

YOUR FREE GIFT IS HERE!

Thank you for purchasing this book. As a token and supplement to your new learnings and personal development journey, you will receive this booklet as a gift, and it's completely free.

This includes - as already announced in this book - a valuable resource of simple approach and actionable ideas to mastermind your own routine towards a more calm and confident way to tackle your everyday.

This booklet will provide you a powerful insight on:

- How to formulate empowering habits that can change your life

- Masterminding your own Power of 3

- Just the 3 things you need to drastically change your life and how you feel about yourself

- How to boost your self-esteem and self-awareness

- Creating a positive feedback loop everyday

You can get the bonus booklet as follows:

To access the secret download page, open a browser window on your computer or smartphone and enter: bonus.gerardshaw.com

You will be automatically directed to the download page.

Please note that this bonus booklet may be available for download for a limited time only.